"This book contains a plethora of helpful rituals and activities to foster and enhance family faith. To my mind, the suggestion to include family business as part of the family rituals—e.g., rotating chores, giving allowances, discussing weekly plans, resolving ongoing problems, giving accolades, and planning future family time—is perhaps the most valuable aspect of the book. That recommendation represents a truly wholistic approach to family spirituality."

Sandra DeGidio, OSM
Author, *Sacraments Alive* and
Prayer Services for the Elderly

"*Make Family Time Prime Time* is a good book for families who want to set aside time each week to grow in faith together. The ideas cover all seasons of the church year and will help families enrich their family faith experience. The authors suggest a variety of activities so that families can choose the ideas that fit their interests. This book will encourage families to spend time together and give them a framework for doing it."

Patricia Mathson
Author, *Seasons and Celebrations*

"In *Make Family Time Prime Time* Denise Yribarren and DeAnn Koestner offer a wide variety of ideas to help families celebrate one another and their faith. These ideas will help even the creatively-challenged. A helpful resource, especially for school-aged families.

Kathleen Finley
Author, *Dear God: Prayers for Families with Children*
and *Our Family Book of Days: A Record through the Years*

"What a wonderful, treasure chest of ideas and activities that are down-to-earth and fun for families with children of all ages! This is an excellent resource for families to experience God's presence in the ordinary events and happenings of daily life. It will help families grow closer to one another and to God. *Make Family Time Prime Time* is a perfect way for parents to spend quality time with their children. It provides an inspiring journey from heart to heart that can deepen unity and harmony in the family. I highly recommend it."

Bridget Mary Meehan
Author, *Prayers, Activities, Celebrations (and More) for Catholic Families*

Make Family Time
PRIME TIME

FUN WAYS TO BUILD FAITH IN YOUR FAMILY

Denise C. Yribarren and DeAnn L. Koestner

TWENTY-THIRD PUBLICATIONS
Mystic, CT 06355

Dedication

What would family time be without a family to celebrate with? Thank you, Jim, Greg, Daniel, and Joe for eagerly participating in lots of activities and projects, and for offering your unique suggestions and perspectives. Very special appreciation to my husband, Andy, whose love and support are always with me. Thanks, too, Mom and Dad, for my childhood memories—rich in love and tradition.

Finally, I am grateful to some wonderful friends who took time to generously share their own families' traditions and ideas: Chris Filbrandt, Cyndi Freed, Eileen Koestner, and Sandi Siedel. Your contributions not only enriched our book, but you are all a source of encouragement in my life.

This book is dedicated to all of you, with love.

DeAnn Koestner

My foremost thanks to my husband, George, who has, without exception, given me the room to pursue the path of self-development and growth. George, thank you for the confidence you've shown in me! To my wonderful children, Hilary, Madelyn, and Emily, thank you for inspiring and collaborating in many of the projects. My gratitude also to my Mom, who planted the seeds of family celebration as she thoughtfully decorated our mantel with seasonal displays as I was growing up.

I truly appreciate the support of my relatives and friends who generously shared their successes and traditions: Jim and Jo Torzala; Kevin and Renee Beanes; Dan and Tina Flahive; Glenn and Yvette Westmoreland; Tom and Mary Coury; Carl and Kathy Heinze; Mike and Kathy Richard; Stormy Beyer and Mary Kerwin; Sam and Mary Ann Yates; Larry and Florence Harrison; Joan Harrison; Ken and Christine Shackel; and Marcy and Walter Meacham.

My gratitude is to all of you!

Denise Yribarren

Twenty-Third Publications
185 Willow Street
P.O. Box 180
Mystic, CT 06355
(860) 536-2611
800-321-0411

ISBN 0-89622-712-X
Library of Congress Catalog Card Number 96-61095
Printed in the U.S.A.

Table of Contents

CHAPTER FOUR

Lent & Easter

CHAPTER FIVE

Celebrations All Year Long

CHAPTER ONE

Our Family Grows in Faith

The activities found in this chapter will help you to explore who you are as a family and who you are as a family of God. What makes your family unique? What Christian traits do you value? How can you grow closer to God? The more families include God in their daily lives, the more both parents and children will see God's pivotal position in their lives.

Family Candle

You will need:

old crayons

2 old pots, one larger than the other, or a double boiler

package of paraffin or wax (you can use old candle stubs, chopped up with wicks removed)

large empty frozen juice can, with lid left on bottom

recycled candle about 5" tall—perhaps one left from Advent or Lent

Have the children take the paper off old crayons and break them into 1/2" pieces. (About one cup of these pieces is needed.) Bring some water to a boil in the larger of two pots. (Fill the bottom pot only so high that the water will not overflow when you put the second pot inside it.) When the water is boiling, turn down the heat to a simmer. Place the paraffin or wax in the second, smaller pot, and put this pot inside the larger one.

Stand the old candle in the center of the juice can and sprinkle the crayon bits around it. Fill the can with crayons, but do not cover the top of the candle.

Carefully pour the melted wax from the pot into the juice can. Be sure not to cover the wick of the old candle. Allow two to three hours for cooling, then gently peel away the juice can.

You can use stick-on letters to add your family's name to the outside of the candle and/or colorful stickers for decoration. Consider making several candles as gifts for aunts, uncles, grandparents, or neighbors at Christmas and other times of celebration.

Your Family Road Map

Create a road map of the important events and happenings in your family's life.

You will need:

    one large sheet of poster board
    copies of the roadway and symbols
       (found on pages 7–8)
    stickers (optional)
    crayons, colored pencils, or markers
    glue

On a piece of blank writing paper, discuss and list chronologically some of the milestone events in your family—marriage, births, moving, first home, pets, schools, special trips, difficulties, and happy times.

Once the list is made, talk a bit about God's presence throughout all these times, whether they were difficult or joyful. Some things that seemed worrisome at the time may have later led to positive occurrences. For example, a job loss could have helped your family to become closer to each other as you explored options and ways to cope with less income. Talk about trusting God,

no matter what life brings. (It would be helpful for parents and older children to give specific examples from their personal experiences.)

To create your road map, trace or photocopy the road pieces and symbols (see pages 7–8), as many of each as you'd like to use. You can also draw your own symbols to represent the events your family listed on the sheet of paper. Color and cut out the road pieces and symbols.

Choose a beginning spot on the poster board and glue down the road pieces to form a route. Then, starting at the beginning, glue on symbols that are appropriate for your family's experiences. (You may want to place these chronologically along the route.) If you wish, add stickers along the way for decoration, and don't forget to fill in the billboards! Make the roadway as simple or detailed as your family desires.

When your family road map is finished, put your family's name at the top and find a place to display it in your home.

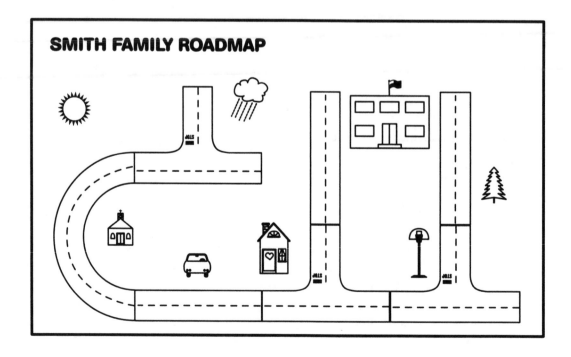

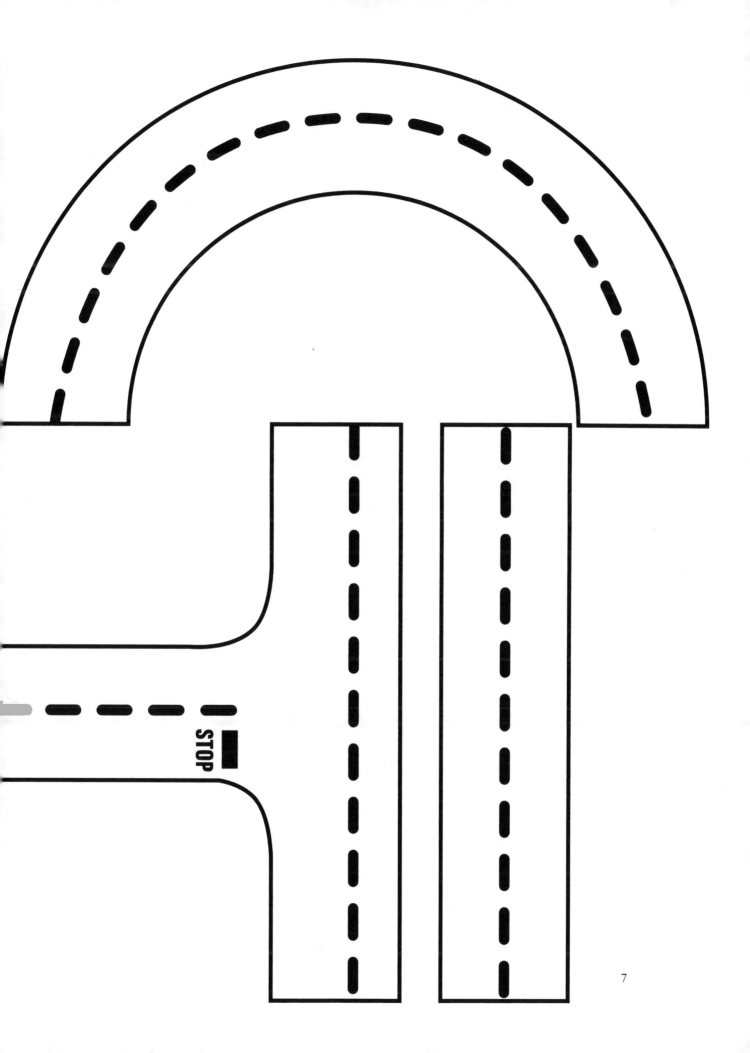

STOP

Fruits of the Spirit

You will need:

Bible
poster board
red construction paper
markers, colored pencils, or crayons
scissors
glue

To begin, find Psalm 1:1–3 and Galatians 5:22 in your Bible, and read these verses aloud to the family. The psalm reading helps to show that living a good and virtuous life is part of God's will for us. The passage from St. Paul's letter describes nine of the fruits of the Holy Spirit, which are ways that we can begin to live as God wants us to live.

Draw a large tree—big enough to hold twelve apples—on the poster board. On the red construction paper, draw 12 apples using the pattern below, or your own cre-

ation. Cut these out (older children can help the younger ones with cutting). On each apple, write one of the twelve fruits of the Holy Spirit: charity, joy, peace, patience, kindness, goodness, endurance, mildness, faithfulness, modesty, self-control, and chastity.

Divide the apples among family members—you may wish to give the adults the apples with the more difficult fruits of the Spirit on them. Talk about what each fruit, or virtue, means and how it can be applied to our lives. Family members can then illustrate their chosen fruits by drawing a simple picture or symbol on each. For instance, kindness might be illustrated with a happy face.

During the week, encourage family members to compliment one another when they see someone practicing one of the fruits of the Spirit.

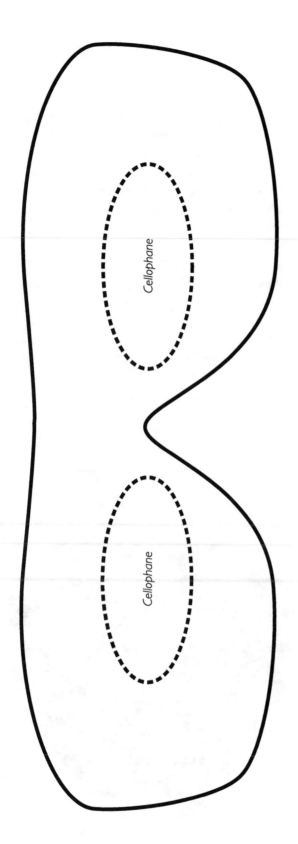

Cellophane

Cellophane

Rose-Colored Glasses

Having faith in God and putting this faith to work means seeing the world with spiritual rather than secular eyes. To illustrate this subtle concept, make masks with the openings covered by rose-colored "lenses."

You will need:

  construction paper or cardboard
  scissors
  markers, crayons, colored pencils
  glitter, stickers, and other decorations
  red or pink cellophane or plastic wrap
  tape
  straws or popsicle sticks

Depending on the ages of your children, you can either draw and cut out the masks using the pattern to the left, or have them do their own designing and cutting. Decorate the masks with markers, glitter, crayons, or stickers.

Cut two pieces of cellophane or plastic wrap to fit over the eye openings on the back side of the mask, and tape them in place. Then, tape one straw or popsicle stick to either side of the mask so the children can hold it up to their face.

As you are working on this project, try to draw older children into a discussion about how our religious beliefs color our lives. When we see things through the eyes of faith, our actions toward one another change, usually for the good.

Talk about how the tinted cellophane doesn't change what you see, but gives a different perspective. Relate this to our faith—Christ doesn't actually change what we observe, but helps to color our interpretation and how we respond to what we see. Parents can further illustrate this with some specific examples from their own lives.

Stained-Glass Window

black construction paper (one sheet for
  each person)
scissors
tape and/or glue
different-colored construction paper
white construction paper
markers

Fold the black paper in half lengthwise.
Round off the two upper corners to form an
arched window shape. Make slits in the
window 1" apart, leaving a frame that is 1"
from the bottom and side edges, and 2"
down from the top (see illustration below).

Cut the construction paper into strips
that are 1" wide and 8 1/2" long. As you
cut, talk about the positive traits a family
should have, such as love, cooperation,
patience, and concern for others. Assign a
trait to each color of construction paper
used for the strips—perhaps red for love,
blue for cooperation, yellow for patience,
and green for concern.

Unfold the black paper window. One by
one, weave the colored strips into the window, starting under one section of the black
and going over the next section, alternating
this way from the bottom to the top. To begin
weaving the second strip, start opposite of the
way you began weaving the first strip, going
over the black first and then under.

Continue alternating strips this way. Work
from the left to the right, pushing each strip
over to the left as far as possible when you
weave. As you are weaving a particular
color, talk about the trait it represents and
discuss ways to show this trait in your family. When each person is done weaving each
color strip into their window, tape or glue
down the ends of the strip inside the top and
bottom edge of the window frame.

When the weaving is done, cut a cross from
the white paper and glue it on the middle of
the window. Write a message on the cross
such as "Jesus loves me" or "I am the way, the
truth, and the life" or "Father, Son and Holy
Spirit." Display the windows in your home.

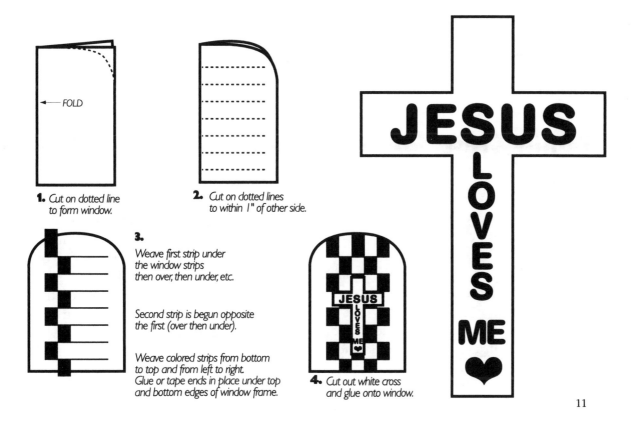

1. Cut on dotted line
to form window.

2. Cut on dotted lines
to within 1" of other side.

3.

Weave first strip under
the window strips
then over, then under, etc.

Second strip is begun opposite
the first (over then under).

Weave colored strips from bottom
to top and from left to right.
Glue or tape ends in place under top
and bottom edges of window frame.

4. Cut out white cross
and glue onto window.

Family Crest

You will need:
crest pattern
cardboard or heavy paper
pencil, markers, or crayons

Celebrate the uniqueness of your family with a family crest. Use the pattern above, or create a crest of your own.

One way to design the crest is to divide the pattern so that it has one section for each family member. Then have everyone illustrate his or her own interests. Or, you may want to use the crest to illustrate one or two themes that represent your family's interests and characteristics. These can be of a spiritual, social, genealogical, recreational, or professional nature. When the crest is completed, hang as is or fasten to a piece of fabric to make a banner.

Sabbath House

You will need:
   cardboard or poster board
   pattern for a house (see page 14)
   crayons, markers, or colored pencils
   scissors
   a sheet of white paper
   tape
   Bible

Ahead of time: On a piece of cardboard or poster board, draw a picture of a house with at least six or seven windows (use the pattern on page 14, or create one of your own). Color and decorate the house, then cut along three sides ONLY of each window, so that it can be folded open (like an Advent calendar).

Tape a piece of white paper behind the house, so that it can be seen inside each window. Open each window, and write down a Scripture passage or activity, choosing from the list that follows or using your own ideas.

For family time: Each family member takes a turn opening a window and reading the message behind it. If a Bible verse appears, have that person locate it in the Bible and read the verse aloud. If an activity appears, then all family members participate in the activity. Continue taking turns until all windows have been opened.

The house can be saved and used over and over for family time—just change the back sheet and use new Scripture verses and activities behind the windows.

Window Ideas:
   Psalms 25:1
   Have a family hug
   Ephesians 6:1
   Sirach 6:15–16
   Matthew 7:12
   Tell about your favorite memory from
      when you were young
   Luke 10:27
   Ephesians 4:32
   Tell about a time you felt close to God
   Sirach 5:8
   Proverbs 16:3
   Sing "Jesus Loves Me" or some other
      favorite religious song
   1 Corinthians 13:4a
   Share cookies with each other

Sabbath Observance

In the Jewish orthodox tradition, the Sabbath is a day reserved for God. It is a day filled with quiet time, reflection, and peace. An absolute minimum of work is performed in order to channel most of one's energy toward God.

You may be thinking that all of the above sounds rather quaint—quite foreign to our fast-paced lives! Yet there is something very appealing and comforting about reserving one day for relaxation and "re-creation." It requires an attitude far different from the one we adopt for the worka-day world, which demands that we constantly produce.

In our homes, we occasionally select certain Sundays to observe a Sabbath time. A few hours or an entire afternoon is set aside for quiet time. Modern conveniences like the television, telephone, stereo, and computer are shut off. Time is spent reading, praying, taking a walk, practicing the piano, writing letters, or playing a game together.

At first, your children may express boredom with the lack of entertainment provided during this quiet time. But slowly, they will begin to participate in the more reflective activities, and in that short period, your family will have spent time coming closer to God and to each other.

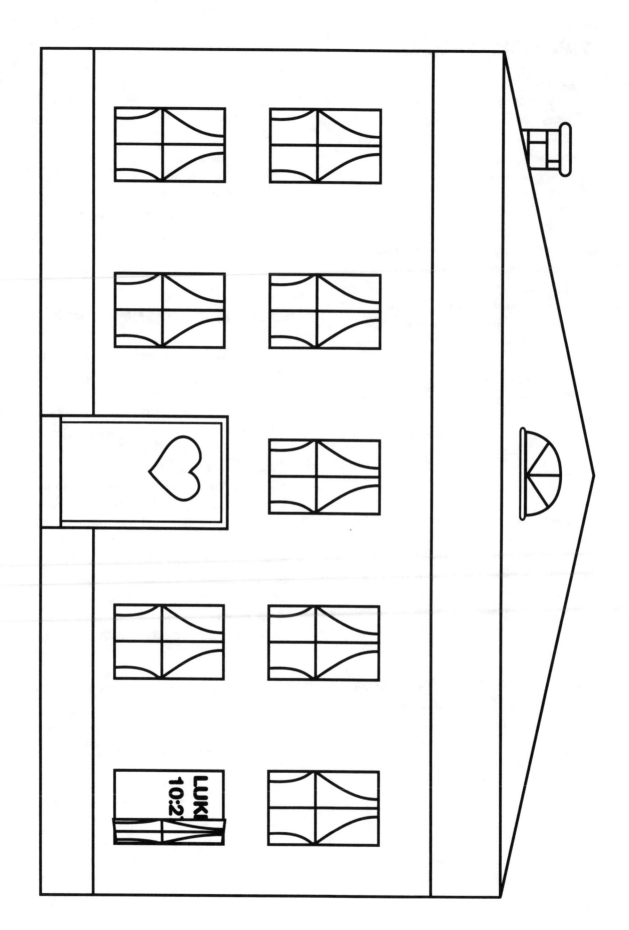

Family Hands

1 1/2 cups table salt
2 1/4 cups hot water
6 cups flour
3 tablespoons vegetable oil
disposable aluminum cookie sheet
rolling pin
tempera paints and paintbrushes

Let the salt dissolve in the hot water. Stir in the flour and oil. Knead this dough well. Spread the dough in the cookie sheet, rolling it flat and smoothing the top with the rolling pin.

Have each family member put their right handprint in the dough. Press the hand in rather hard, especially the fingertips. (If your family is large, double the recipe and use two sheets or a bigger disposable sheet.)

Bake the handprints in a 300-degree oven for 1 1/2 to 2 hours. Let this dry at least overnight. When thoroughly dry, have each family member paint or write their name next to (or inside) their handprint. They should then add one or two qualities that make them unique in the family; for example, a sunny smile, a happy disposition, kind words for everyone, and the like. You can then decorate the rest of the "mural," and display on a plate stand.

Variation: Next to their name, have each family member write one way they can be a "helping hand" to others in the family.

Do I Know You?

You will need:

paper
pencils

As a family, brainstorm to come up with a list of questions on various topics. Some possibilities include: What famous person do you admire most? What is your favorite color? Would you choose chocolate or vanilla ice cream? Which sport do you enjoy playing most? Where in the United States would you like to travel?

Divide family members into two teams with one person being the moderator. Send one person from each team to another room. The moderator chooses one of the questions. The team members that are left must answer the questions as they think their "missing" team member would.

Ask three questions and get three answers before the team members are brought back into the room. Each of them is then asked the same three questions. Give one point for each answer that matches what their teammates said. When all three questions have been answered, choose a new moderator and send another set of team members out of the room. Repeat question and answer process as above, until everyone has had a chance to be the ones out of the room

(You might enjoy playing this game with extended family members, another family, or good friends.)

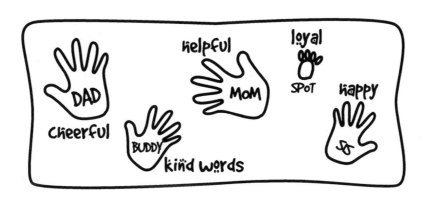

Other Family Activities

•During your family time or at dinner one night, have each family member talk about the time when he or she felt closest to God.

•Mom or Dad can hide a penny or holy card under one dinner plate before the family sits down to dinner. Whoever finds the penny under their plate can say grace for that meal. (They also get to keep the card or penny!)

•Give each child their own "Jesus Bank." (You can make them from various containers—empty frosting tubs work well—or purchase banks at a religious store.) Each week the children put a portion of their allowance in the bank. After saving a while, they can donate their funds to a charity they choose (St. Vincent de Paul Society, food banks, a homeless shelter, and the like). You can also do this activity as a family.

•Try having a "monk meal" once a week. To do this, everyone eats dinner in silence while listening to classical or other appropriate music. The silent meal can be followed by an evening without television. The family can play a game together or read a book aloud.

•Check with your church office or parish manager. Is there some repair work or painting at church your family could do? Could your family plant some flowers or do some weeding? Try gathering together and cleaning the actual sanctuary before services. Perhaps, as a family, you could help with childcare on a regular basis, or provide senior citizens with transportation to services and functions.

•Pastors work, often round-the-clock, for the good of the parish, receiving little or no thanks. As a family, shop for and/or bake a basket of goodies (cookies, nuts, coffee, and the like) for your pastor. Include a homemade card of appreciation.

You could also invite the pastor or other members of the parish staff over for dinner one evening or Sunday afternoon. This can offer an opportunity to get to know these people in an informal and relaxed setting.

16

CHAPTER TWO

Scripture

Becoming familiar with Scripture through games, puzzles, or art projects makes it a fun and challenging experience for everyone. The activities that follow will help parents, as well as children, add to their understanding and knowledge of the people and words of God found within the Bible.

P.S. Do you know what all the numbers and words mean when you see a reference to a Bible passage? Here's how it works; let's take Genesis 6:14–16 as an example. The name "Genesis," in this case, is the book of the Bible where the passage will be found (there are 46 books in the Old Testament and 27 books in the New Testament, four of which are the gospels of Matthew, Mark, Luke, and John); the first number, "6" in the example, refers to the chapter in that book (chapters are usually noted in the Bible with big numbers); and the number(s) following the colon refer to the verse(s), which are short phrases or sentences marked by small numbers within the chapter.

Bible Charades

You will need:
Bible or Bible storybook
paper and pencils
scissors
props (optional)

Make a list of some favorite Bible stories, preferably ones that are familiar and have some action in them. Cut the list into separate strips, then fold and put the strips into an empty bowl or box.

Have each family member choose one of the strips and then play charades. To do this, the person must act out the story on the piece of paper he or she chose, while the others try to guess what the story is.

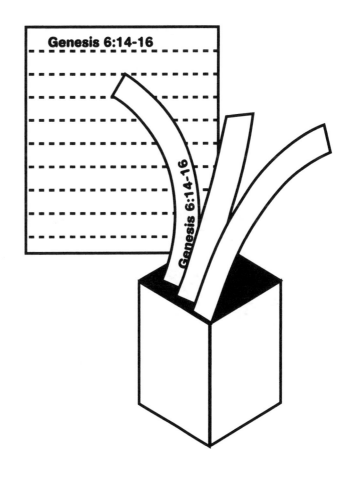

Bible Concentration

You will need:
Bible or Bible storybook
poster board
pencil
ruler
scissors
markers, crayons, or colored pencils

To make the playing cards:
Divide the poster board into 2" or 3" squares, depending on how big you want your cards to be, or use a regular playing card as a pattern. Draw an even number of squares on the poster board—between thirty and forty is good—then cut these out.

As a family, brainstorm to find symbols from familiar Old Testament and New Testament stories that could be drawn on the cards. Some examples include: apple, snake, or fig leaf (Adam and Eve); rainbow, ark, rain, or pair of animals (Noah); ram (Abraham and Isaac); ladder (Jacob); coat of many colors, wheat (Joseph); a burning bush, commandment tablets, staff (Moses); harp or flute (David); crown (Solomon); lily (Mary); hammer or saw (Jesus' father, Joseph); cross (Jesus); dove (Holy Spirit); church, rock (Peter).

After compiling a list of fifteen to twenty symbols (think of enough for half the cards you've cut out), let each person take a few pairs of cards. Divide the list of symbols among everyone, giving each person a symbol for each pair of cards he or she has. Draw and color the symbols, making sure that each symbol is drawn on two cards to form a pair.

Playing the game:
Shuffle all the cards and place them face down in rows. In turn, each person then flips over two cards, trying to find a matching pair. If the two cards do match, that person gets to take another turn and flip over two more cards. If they don't match, the cards are turned back over and play goes to the next person. Play until all matches have been made.

Bible Crossword

You will need:

Bible or Bible storybook
graph paper
pencils

Design your own crossword puzzle using words from Bible stories. Make it easy or hard, depending on the ages of your children. Construct the puzzle on graph paper, and write clues for each of the words.

You can also use the puzzle below that was created by Denise's daughter Hilary. (The answer key is on page 99.)

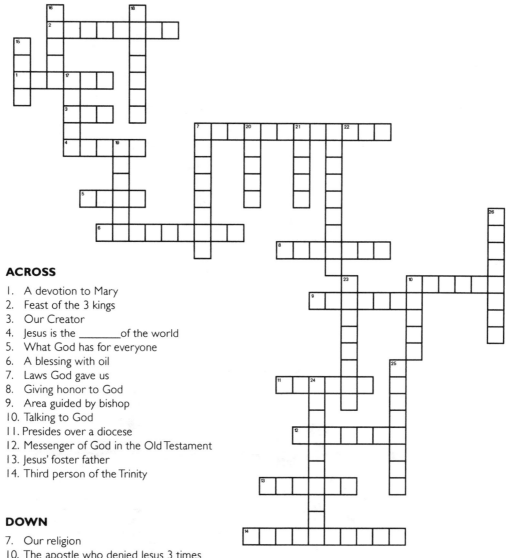

ACROSS

1. A devotion to Mary
2. Feast of the 3 kings
3. Our Creator
4. Jesus is the _____ of the world
5. What God has for everyone
6. A blessing with oil
7. Laws God gave us
8. Giving honor to God
9. Area guided by bishop
10. Talking to God
11. Presides over a diocese
12. Messenger of God in the Old Testament
13. Jesus' foster father
14. Third person of the Trinity

DOWN

7. Our religion
10. The apostle who denied Jesus 3 times
15. Jesus' mother
16. Son of God
17. God's winged messenger
18. Mary's angel
19. God's kingdom
20. Loving care or forgiveness
21. Boy who challenges Goliath
22. Holy Communion
23. A calling from God
24. Outward signs instituted by Christ to give grace
25. Jesus' 12 special disciples
26. Jesus was raised here

Noah and the Rainbow

You will need:

  Bible or Bible storybook
  white construction paper or cardboard
  crayons, markers, colored pencils
  string
  dowel or wire hanger

Read the story of Noah in Genesis 6:5–9:17, or read a version of this story from a Bible storybook.

Give each person a piece of white paper or cardboard, and have them draw a rainbow on it, filling up the paper as much as possible. Color the rainbow using crayons, markers, or colored pencils. (You could also cut several colors of construction paper into small squares, and glue these on in a mosaic pattern to form the colors of the rainbow.)

When everyone has colored their rainbow, take a black marker and write one of the key phrases from the story of Noah on each person's rainbow. Some suggestions are: "Noah found favor in the sight of the Lord" (6:8); "You shall bring two of every kind into the ark" (6:19); "The rain fell on the earth forty days and forty nights" (7:12); "God said, 'I will never again curse the ground because of humankind'" (8:21); "Be fruitful and multiply, and fill the earth" (9:1); "I am establishing a covenant with you and your descendants after you" (9:9).

Take the completed rainbows, and make a small slit near the top with a scissor edge, or use a hole punch. Tie a string through the top of each one. Hang the rainbows from the dowel or hanger to make a mobile. Be sure everyone understands that the rainbow is a sign of God's promise that the earth would never again be destroyed by a flood.

Joseph's Coat of Many Colors

You will need:

    Bible

    large brown grocery bags

    scissors

    items for coloring and decorating, such as: glitter, fabric trim, ribbons, paint, markers, crayons, construction paper

    glue

Read the story of Joseph and his brothers (Genesis 37). Talk about the feelings the brothers displayed towards Joseph, their younger brother. Ask the children if they have ever experienced jealous, angry, or upset feelings toward anyone. Share some times you have felt these feelings, too. Talk about how Joseph's brothers later changed their feelings and how Joseph showed them forgiveness.

Give each person a paper bag, and turn it upside down with the bottom (closed) end of the bag facing up. Now cut straight up the front of the bag, from bottom to top. Continue cutting from the front opening, and make an oval shape in the top of the bag for a neck opening. Next, cut out two armhole openings, one in each side of the bag. (Adults or older children help younger children cut out the openings.)

Use construction paper, paint, markers, glitter, or fabric trim to make the "coats" many-colored.

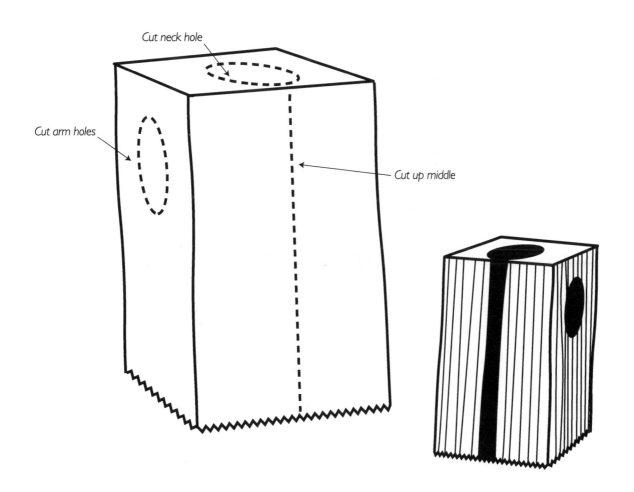

Cut neck hole

Cut arm holes

Cut up middle

21

Daniel and the Lions

You will need:
   Bible or Bible storybook
   small paper plates (brown, if possible)
   brown, red, and black construction paper
   glue
   scissors
   black marker

Read the story of Daniel in the lion's den in Daniel 6:6–28 or from a Bible storybook. Talk about how dangerous it was for Daniel to follow God at that time in history. Discuss why it is easier to be a Christian today, and some ways that it may be harder. Use some examples from your everyday life.

To make the lion, take a paper plate and fringe the edges all around with about 1/2" slits. Cut ears, eyes, nose, and whiskers from construction paper. Glue these on the plate to make the lion's face—a mouth shape can be drawn under the nose. Cut out a lion's body from brown construction paper using the pattern on the next page as a guide; or, simply cut an oval for the body, and four legs and a tail that can be glued to the body. Glue the lion's body to the head, and write on the body "TRUST IN THE LORD."

TRUST IN
THE LORD

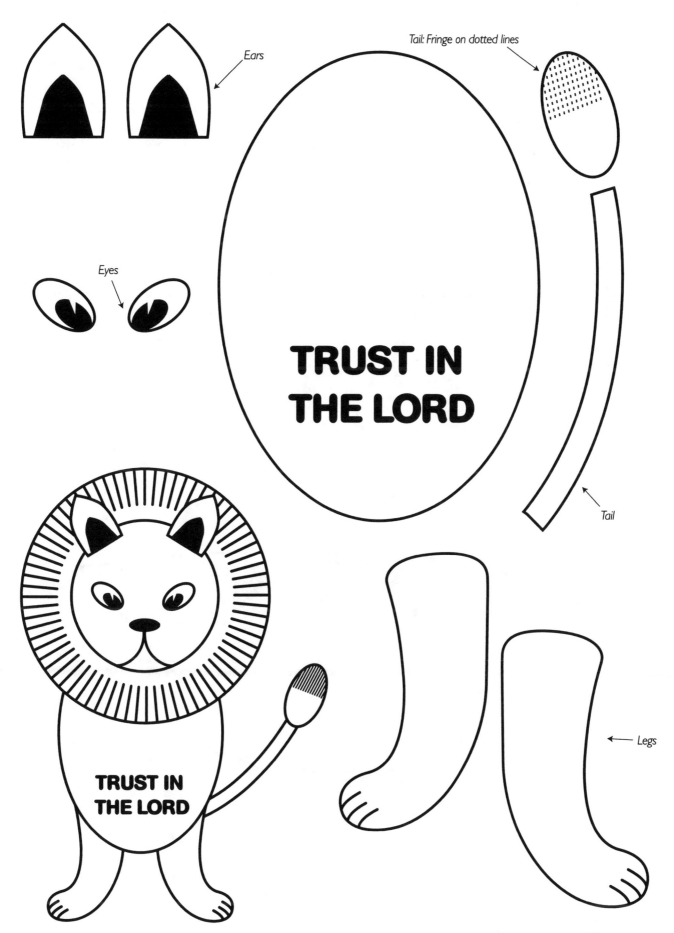

Ears

Tail: Fringe on dotted lines

Eyes

Tail

Legs

TRUST IN
THE LORD

TRUST IN
THE LORD

Light of the World

You will need:
Bible
cardboard or poster board
two star shapes, one large, one small
scissors or craft knife
tape
yellow tissue paper or cellophane

To begin, read aloud a Scripture passage that talks about light. Some suggestions are Psalm 18:28–30, Wisdom 18:1–4, Matthew 5:14–16, John 1:1–9, and Acts 13:47.

Next, trace the large star pattern (one star for each person), onto the board, and cut out the stars. Then trace the smaller star shape in the middle of the larger ones. Cut this smaller star out (younger children may need help with this cutting).

Place a piece of the yellow tissue or cellophane over this star opening and tape into place. Turn the large star over and write "We are the light of the world" on it. (You can also use a verse from one of the Scripture passages you read earlier.) Hang the stars in a sunny window and watch the light shine through!

24

Abraham's Stars

You will need:

Bible
yellow or blue paper
black marker
glue
silver or clear glitter
string
hanger or dowel

Read aloud Genesis 15:1–6 and talk about God's promise to Abram (later called Abraham). Remind everyone that Abraham is considered the father of the Hebrew race, and therefore, our own ancestral father.

Cut seven stars out of the colored paper, in whatever size you wish. Write the following phrase in black marker on the stars, one word on each star: "Your children will number as the stars." Then take a paintbrush, and wipe a thin layer of glue over each star. Now gently sprinkle glitter over the glue (be careful not to block out the words). String the stars together and attach to the hanger or dowel to form a mobile.

Later, if it is a clear night, go outside and gaze at the stars. Try to count them all.

Scripture Ladder

As Jacob begins a journey from his father's house to a new life, he has a dream showing him a ladder reaching to the heavens. In that dream, Jacob was given God's blessing and assurance that God would be with him on his journey. In this activity, your family will build a "ladder" that will help bring you closer to God by memorizing key Scripture passages.

You will need:

one 24" dowel, cut in half
24 popsicle sticks
glue or a glue gun
fine-tipped permanent marker
Bible

Begin by having a family member read aloud Genesis 28:1–17, the story of Jacob's dream. To construct the ladder, lay down the two dowel pieces parallel to each other, the length of a popsicle stick apart. Beginning at the bottom of the dowels, glue the first popsicle stick in place. Then add the next stick, about 1/4" away, and another until you reach the top of the dowels.

(See illustration on the following page.) Turn the ladder over, and glue down popsicle sticks along the backside, following the same pattern as on the front. Let dry.

Choose one Scripture passage from the list on the following page that everyone in the family can memorize. Write the passage on the first rung. (A good time to learn and practice the passages is after a shared meal.) At the end of each week, have everyone say the passage aloud, then talk about what it may mean in their lives. Talk about how this passage shows that God is near to us in our everyday lives.

Do the same every week, until you come to the top of the front side of the ladder. Then take the family out for an ice cream cone or other such treat to celebrate. The following week, turn the ladder over and begin again. (The selections listed on page 26 are in the order in which they appear in the Bible, but feel free to use them in any sequence you'd like.)

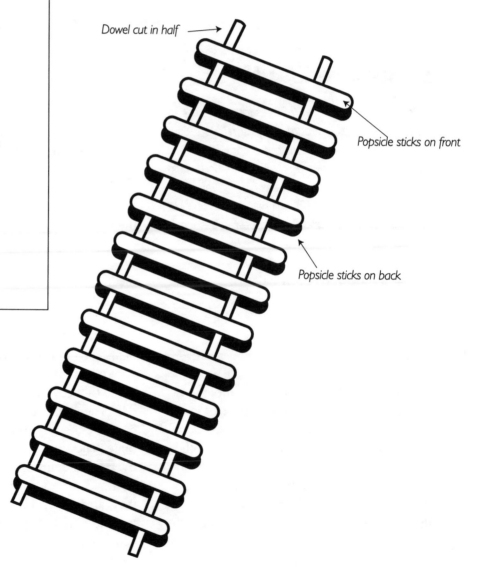

Dowel cut in half

Popsicle sticks on front

Popsicle sticks on back

CHAPTER THREE

Advent, Christmas & Epiphany

On the pages that follow you'll find activities and traditions for the Christmas season, from Advent through the Epiphany. Some may become favorites for your family as they have been for ours. Try a few of these this year, save a few for next, or add some activities to the traditions and customs already in place in your home.

Before you begin...

The Christmas season—which begins with Advent and ends with the Epiphany—is rich with tradition and activities. This is one time of the year that most families have traditions, celebrations, and customs which they observe.

Yet often, the very fullness of this season means families may find themselves too overwhelmed with "doing," leaving little time for the quieter, simpler "waiting" moments of Advent.

Obviously, accomplishing as much as possible prior to the holidays can help keep them from being so stressful. Preparation and selection go a long way toward making holiday times less hectic and more enjoyable. Here are a few suggestions to ease the rushed, too-much-to-do feelings common during December:

• Set aside three days during Advent which the whole family can devote to working together. Designate one day for baking, one for wrapping gifts, and one for decorating.

• Double the quantity of your meals where possible and freeze the extras for easy meals on those days when the "to do" list is too long.

• Try giving practical gifts this year instead of searching for that elusive "perfect" gift. Postage stamps, phone cards, or food staples are just a few ideas.

• Be selective! Don't feel you must do a Jesse tree, an Advent calendar, an Advent wreath, and make your own wrapping paper all in one year. Choosing to do one or two rituals each year not only keeps the activities fresh and new, it also allows you to concentrate more fully on the ones you have chosen.

As a family, decide how you want to spend your Advent and Christmas season, and plan accordingly. Identify the special rituals and customs you and your children would like to participate in. Focus on the entire season. Celebrate St. Nicholas Day, the Epiphany, and the Marian feasts. Limit parties and outings during the month, especially the ones that don't involve the whole family. Forgo random television viewing and choose only the shows that will enhance the season.

Advent Chain

You will need:

cardboard or poster board
21-28 strips of colored paper, 1" by 8"
stapler or glue

On the board, trace and cut out the star on the following page. Copy the poem in the center. Next, count the number of days from the first Sunday of Advent to Christmas Eve. You will need that many strips of paper for your chain.

As a family, think up activities that you can do together, one for each day of Advent. (You'll find some suggestions further on.) Jot these down on a sheet of scrap paper.

Take the colored paper strips and number them on one side, using one strip for each day of Advent. On the other side of the strip, write down one activity to do on that day. (Have your planning calendar handy when assigning activities to the numbered strips. An easier activity can be matched to a busy day, and an involved activity can be assigned to a relatively free day.)

Keeping the strips in numerical order, form a paper chain by stapling or gluing the ends of each strip together. Attach the chain with the number "1" on it to the bottom of the star, and hang in a prominent place.

On the first Sunday of Advent, tear the strip with the last number off the chain. (The numbers will tell how many days are left until Christmas.) Sometime during that day, do the activity listed on the strip together as a family. As the chain gets smaller, Christmas draws closer.

Suggested Activities:

- Fill some Christmas stockings for children at a homeless shelter.
- Take an evening walk or drive to enjoy the Christmas lights.
- Read the Christmas story in the Bible (Luke 2:1–21) and let the children act it out.
- Read the story "The Littlest Angel" or O. Henry's "Gift of the Magi."
- Make homemade cards for special people like grandparents and teachers.
- Using shelf paper and rubber stamps, create unique Christmas wrap.
- String popcorn and hang on trees outside for the birds.
- Make paper snowflakes.
- Make a Christmas ornament.
- Start a big jigsaw puzzle.
- Draw names and do something special all week for your secret person.
- Fix a basket of goodies and share with a neighbor.
- Go to a shopping mall and participate in one of the Christmas service activities they offer.
- Sing carols at a nursing home.
- Have an overnight campout by the Christmas tree.

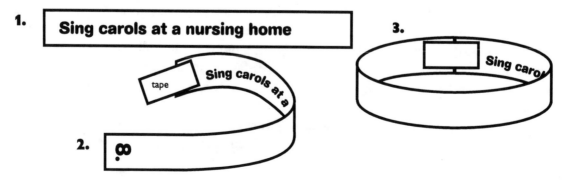

Our Christmas star holds
Special things for us to do.
Remove one link each day
And share its activity, too.
As our chain grows smaller,
Christ's birthday draws near.
Let's spread his peace & love
Throughout the whole year.

Hanukkah

You will need:

    menorah, or picture of one
    candles
    dreidel
    chocolate coins

Hanukkah is not a "Jewish Christmas," but rather a completely different celebration of God's presence in the lives of our fore-bears, the Hebrew people. Understanding the significance of Hanukkah can help families appreciate the richness of tradition in Judaism.

When we first decided to introduce a Hanukkah celebration to our families, we called a nearby temple and asked for their help. The rabbi's assistant was generous with information and told us where we could purchase a menorah (eight-cupped candleholder with a ninth cup for the *shamash*, the candle used to light the other eight), candles, dreidel (children's spinning top), and some chocolate coins. If you have Jewish friends or neighbors, perhaps they can lend you some of these items or give you information on how to obtain them.

To begin your family time, read 1 Maccabees 4:52–59. You can then further relate how Hebrew tradition holds that around 165 BC, the Syrians attacked the Hebrew lands and destroyed the Temple. As the Jews went through the ruins, they found a one-day supply of oil. They used this to burn their lamps, and miraculously, the oil lasted for eight days. The Hebrew people saw this as a sign from God that the small group of faithful Jews would be victorious over the Syrians, and would be free to practice their faith.

Next, light the eight candles of the menorah, which represent the eight days that the oil burned. (During the actual observance of Hanukkah, one candle is lit each day for a period of eight days.) Then, have everyone take turns spinning the dreidel. Give out the chocolate coins as prizes to the person who guesses on which side the dreidel will land. End the evening by sharing the chocolate coins, which symbolize good luck.

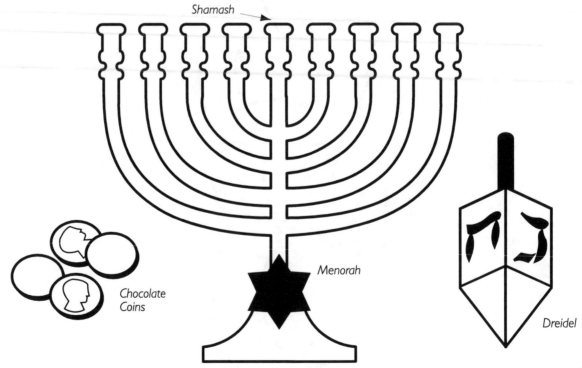

Shamash

Chocolate Coins

Menorah

Dreidel

Waiting for Jesus

You will need:

> empty doll cradle or crib, or shoebox
>   made to look like a crib
> candles
> doll, about 10" long
> white cloth to wrap the doll in

On the first Sunday of Advent, put the empty doll cradle or decorated shoebox out in the room where your Christmas tree will go. (You can make a shoebox crib as part of a family time activity.) Leave it there throughout Advent.

After dinner on Christmas Eve, gather the younger members of the family in one of the bedrooms. Give each of the children, except one, a candle and help them light it. The children then carry their lighted candles out to the empty crib, while the chosen child carries "baby Jesus" (the doll wrapped in white cloth). The baby is then placed in the empty crib. To close this ritual, read a Christmas story and/or sing a few carols together.

Gifts of Love

Spend a family evening in November or December preparing small, thoughtful gifts for neighbors, family, and/or friends. Some ideas include: filling a box with Christmas wrap and bows; making homemade Christmas paper by dipping cookie cutters in tempera paint and placing them on brown butcher paper; putting a few samples of special coffee in a new coffee mug; filling a basket with ribbon, tags, and scotch tape; baking some loaves of homemade bread; and making some fudge or Christmas candy to box and give away.

Christmas Letter

You will need:

> Bible
> letter-size paper
> a pencil or pen

During November, choose a psalm or other Bible quote that relates to the spirit of Christmas. Some suggestions are Isaiah 9:2, Isaiah 52:7, Psalm 98:3, Psalm 128:1, Titus 2:11, or choose a verse from Luke 2:6–20. Design a Christmas border around the edges of a piece of letter paper featuring the verse your family has chosen.

Use this border to frame a Christmas greeting or letter from your family. Type your message on the framed sheet, then make as many copies of it as needed. You can also have the children color the border on each of the letters as an extra personal touch.

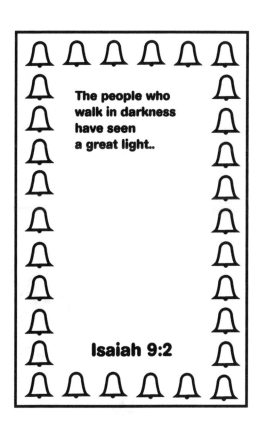

The people who walk in darkness have seen a great light..

Isaiah 9:2

Christmas Banner

You will need:

an 18" by 18" piece of red fabric

12" by 12" fabric squares (felt works well) in each of the following colors: green, yellow, and white

needle and thread, or glue

tracing paper

scissors

fabric paint, preferably glittery

sequins

24" dowel

string or ribbon to hang banner

To attach pictures to banner, you can use:

iron-on backing (about a yard), fabric glue, or a glue gun

In this activity, you will make a Christmas banner to celebrate Jesus' presence among us. Turn down 3/4" along the upper edge of the piece of red fabric, and stitch or glue down the edge to form a casing for the dowel.

(If you are going to use iron-on backing to attach your shapes to the banner, follow the directions on the package and adhere the backing to each of the three fabric squares before you cut out the shapes. Also, letters must be traced in reverse when using iron-on backing.)

Trace the patterns for the shapes (see page 33) and letters (see patterns on pages 101–103). On the green fabric, trace the tree; on the yellow, a few stars; and on the white, the letters for the word "Rejoice." Trace a few packages on whatever scraps of fabric remain. Once all the tracing is done, carefully cut out the shapes and letters.

If you are using iron-on backing, peel off the paper on all pieces and arrange them on your banner in whatever way your family wishes. Preheat the iron to the steam setting, and iron down the shapes and letters in place.

If you are using fabric glue or a glue gun, lay the banner down on a flat surface, and arrange the shapes and letters on it as you wish. Then attach with glue, piece by piece. Let the glue dry before proceeding.

Once they are attached to the banner, decorate the tree and packages using the paint and sequins. Discuss as a family what gifts God has given your family and gifts your family wishes to pass on during this Christmas season. Use fabric paint to write your gift ideas on the packages.

Let the banner dry flat for several hours, then attach a string or ribbon to the dowel and hang the banner in your home. You may wish to sing or play a tape of "O come, O come Emmanuel" as your family chooses a place for your special banner.

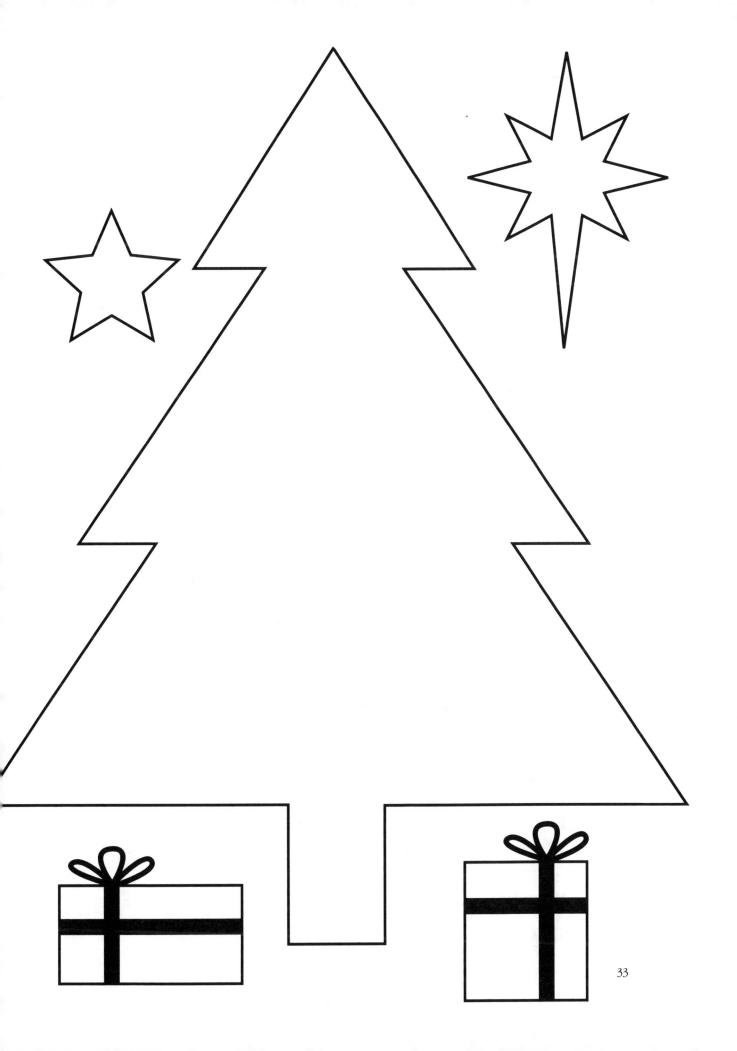

33

Christmas Ornaments

You will need:
1 1/2 cups table salt
2 1/4 cups hot water
6 cups flour
3 tablespoons vegetable oil

Many families purchase a new ornament for their tree each year. This year, try fashioning your own homemade ornaments. These clay ornaments are fun to make; afterwards, you can paint them with a thin coat of varnish or acrylic for durability.

Let the salt dissolve in the hot water. Stir in the flour and oil. Knead this dough well. Spread the dough on a wooden board or cookie sheet, rolling it flat and smoothing the top with the rolling pin.

Cut Christmas shapes out of the dough with a cookie cutter or paring knife. You can also mold the dough into three-dimensional figures. Make a little hole at the top of each shape for hanging.

Bake the ornaments in a 300-degree oven for 1 1/2 to 2 hours. Take out of the oven, and let dry at least overnight. When thoroughly dry, decorate the ornaments with poster paint, glitter, and anything else your creativity desires.

Almost Gingerbread Houses

You will need:
single serving milk cartons, empty and clean
foil
cardboard pieces
graham crackers
frosting (canned or homemade)
decorations: cereal, candies, coconut, etc.

Place the milk carton on some foil-covered cardboard. Cover the sides of the carton with graham crackers as "panels," using the frosting as a glue. Use more graham crackers or square-shaped cereal for the roof. Decorate with coconut (snow) and various candies. (Hint: Children should have a healthy and filling meal or snack before starting this project! Also, allow plenty of time for them to create their houses.)

Twelve Days of Christmas

Most families experience some letdown after the festivities of Christmas Day. To offset this, plan (sometime in Advent) an activity for each of the twelve days following Christmas, and culminating on the feast of the Epiphany. Here are some ideas:

Movie night: rent or go to a family movie.

Game night: each child chooses a favorite game to play; start with the choice of the youngest.

Exchange night: the children make dinner (or choose a place to order out from, if cooking would be a risk!), plan the evening activity, and then tuck their parents into bed.

Outside day: plan to spend a few hours outside, whether taking a walk or doing some weather-appropriate activities. Save this day for a weekend so everyone in the family can participate.

Baking day: bake a bread or make a casserole to share with a neighbor or friend.

Thank-you note day: send notes to everyone who gave you and the children a Christmas gift. (Consider having a tasty dessert to encourage everyone to work on these notes.)

No television day: try to go one whole day without watching any television shows or videos.

Backwards day: have pizza for breakfast, eat dessert first at lunch, and then fix pancakes or eggs for supper.

School papers day: since this time is almost halfway through the school year, sort through all the papers that have been saved, and choose the best ones to keep.

Art day: choose clay, paints, or a coloring activity to do today.

Agape night: after dinner, have a mini-prayer service. Use a special cup or glass filled with grape juice or wine, and a small loaf of bread or a roll. Break the bread and pass around, then pass the cup around.

If you'd like, before dinner your family can make a poster or banner on brown butcher paper which reads "Bless our family," and place it near the dinner table.

Epiphany Procession

You will need:
11" by 17" paper or cardboard
scissors
glue
glitter, sequins, paint (for decorating)
boxes
foil wrapping paper
tape or stapler

Have each child make a crown and decorate it with the glitter, sequins, and paint. (You can use the pattern below for the middle section of the crown, and extend the ends to fit the head size of each child.)

Tape or staple it to fit. Next, ask each child to think of a gift they can bring to Jesus, one that doesn't cost money. Have the children write their gift on a piece of paper and put it into one of the boxes. Each child then wraps his or her gift.

When everyone has finished, have the children wear their crowns and process through the house carrying their gifts. Play or sing "We Three Kings of Orient Are" during the procession. End at the Nativity scene, where the children can then unwrap their gifts and tell everyone what they gave to the baby Jesus.

Other Advent & Christmas Activities:

•In late November or on the first Sunday of Advent, put together an Advent wreath (or revitalize the one from last year). Make plans for saying Advent prayers, and assign various family members different days. Allow your Advent wreath to serve as a constant and visible reminder that Advent is a time of waiting for Jesus.

•On December 5th, the eve of St. Nicholas Day, put a shoe outside each bedroom door. Parents can place a small "pummel"—German slang for "little present"—in the shoes to be found the next morning. As the children get older, take turns having one of them be in charge of getting the pummels for everyone and leaving them in the shoes.

•Honor Mary in a special way on the Feast of the Immaculate Conception (December 8th) and on the Feast of Our Lady of Guadalupe (December 12). Gather together to say the rosary or sing a Marian hymn at the end of dinner.

•Buy everyone in the family a new nightgown or pajamas to be worn on Christmas Eve. This gift symbolizes the "newness" of the baby Jesus, as well as the warmth and security a family can offer.

•Before lighting the tree for the first time, say a "Blessing of the Christmas Tree." Use the following one or compose one of your own:

Lord, you created this lovely tree to provide us with shelter and beauty. May this festive tree grace our home and serve as a reminder of your presence during this holy season. Amen.

•Give each child a unique ornament in their stocking at Christmas. At the end of the season when the tree is being taken down, each child puts his or her ornaments away in their own labeled box.

When it's time to decorate next year's tree, the children first hang all the ornaments from their own boxes before putting up the ones that belong to the whole family. (When your children leave home, the set of ornaments can go with them.) Keep a list in each child's box, writing down the ornament, the year it was given, and who gave it to them.

•As Jesus received three gifts from the Wise Men, so some families symbolically give their children three presents at Christmas. (This is a wonderful way to cut down on some of the commercial nature of Christmas, and focus on what is really important to the season.)

•Give an annual "baby shower" for Jesus, with gifts that will be donated to a homeless shelter or food pantry. Invite other families to participate in the "shower"; you may want to have a potluck brunch or dinner along with this activity. Encourage your children to participate by using their own money to buy a gift for Jesus' shower.

•Set a crown on a plate and pile foil-covered candy high in the center for a "Three Kings' Day" treat. At dinner that evening, talk about the gifts family members can give to others which don't cost any money. End by feasting on the candies for dessert.

•Leave your Nativity set up until the feast of the Epiphany (traditionally celebrated on January 6, but liturgically celebrated on the second Sunday after Christmas). On Christmas Day, put the three Wise Men and their camels at a distance from the manger, moving them closer and closer each day until they reach the baby Jesus on the feast of Epiphany.

CHAPTER FOUR

Lent and Easter

The word "lent" comes from the Middle English "lente," and refers to the lengthening of days that comes in springtime. In the early days of the church, Lent was a time of preparation for those who were going to be baptized Christians. These catechumens, as they were called, along with the rest of the Christian community, fasted for forty days—from Ash Wednesday to Holy Saturday, excluding Sundays—in imitation of Jesus' forty-day fast in the desert.

This chapter focuses on ways that your family can grow together through prayer and activities during the lenten and Easter seasons. How appropriate if we could make this spiritual season one of springtime for our own families, a time of growth and development, of hope and new beginnings.

Lenten Calendar

Many of us use Advent calendars, so why not try a Lent calendar? This project takes some initial preparation and work, but once made, it can be used from year to year.

You will need:

a large piece of fabric
several scrap pieces of fabric or felt
40 buttons
needle and thread, or sewing machine
glue gun or fabric glue
colored paper
hole punch
string or thin ribbon for hanging
wooden dowel

Sew a narrow casing at the top of the banner for a dowel to slip through. If desired, you can also sew some trim along the top edge of the banner. Fashion a tree branch with several limbs out of fabric or felt, and glue it onto the background.

Glue or sew the buttons onto the branches (buttons that have a shank underneath work well), leaving enough space around the edge of each button to hang a paper flower on. Cut a 6" by 6" square out of felt or sturdy fabric. Glue down the bottom and two side edges of the fabric onto the banner to form a pocket.

Using the patterns on page 40 or fashioning your own designs, cut out a total of forty pieces from various colored papers. (This will give you enough items for each of the days of Lent, excluding either Sundays or Holy Week.) Punch a hole near the top of each of these. On the back of each piece write a simple practice that everyone in the family can do. (A list of ideas is included below.) Place the forty pieces in the pocket on the banner.

Each morning during Lent, choose one of the flowers from the pocket and read aloud the practice on the back. This will be the family's lenten act for the day. After everyone has heard the action read, hang the flower on one of the buttons, either by slipping the hole over the button (if the button is small enough), or by tying a short string through the hole in the flower and hanging the string on the button.

To finish the banner for Easter, cut out letters for the word "Alleluia" (see letter patterns on pages 101–103) from the fabric scraps. On Holy Saturday, glue these to the top of the banner. Hang the banner in a prominent place in your home as a reminder of how your lenten deeds have brought you to the celebration of Easter.

Variation: If you don't have a lot of buttons in the house, you can forgo them and simply glue the flower onto the tree branch after you have read aloud the lenten action for the day.

Ideas for lenten practices:

- Say a prayer for someone who is sick.
- Share lots of smiles today.
- Go through your closet and find some clothes in good shape to give away.
- Do something helpful for a teacher, parent, or child.
- List five blessings you have been given.
- Read Psalm 100.

- Give up television today.
- Write a family letter to someone who might be lonely.
- Give up snacks for one day.
- Buy a can of food to give to a food bank or homeless shelter.
- Give a hug to everyone in your family.
- Compliment each person in your family sometime today.
- Take an evening walk together and thank God for the moon and stars.
- At one meal today, eat only bread and drink only water. Remember that Jesus is the "Bread of Life."
- At dinner, say a thank-you chain prayer where each person mentions something or someone they are thankful for.
- Do someone else's chores for them.
- At dinner, have each person tell why every family member is special.
- Pray for the homeless, and think about ways your family might help them.
- Do ten jumping jacks and thank God for good health.
- Give up complaining, frowns, and negative thoughts today.
- Make an Easter card for someone.
- Listen to religious music during dinner.
- Read the Easter story from the Bible.
- Pray for a forgiving heart and ask someone to forgive you.
- Make this _____(your child's name) special day. Have everyone do his or her chores and be extra nice to him or her today. (Do this for each of your children on different days.)

Lenten Cross

The lenten cross is a symbolic way to mark the weeks of Lent, much as we mark Advent with a wreath of candles. It is a good way to connect the two seasons of Christmas and Easter.

The tradition of the lenten cross comes from the early days of Christianity. The faithful would save the trunk of the family's Christmas tree, let the wood season over the winter months, and as the time for Lent neared, cut the rough trunk into two pieces. These were then attached to each other to form a cross, and six candles were placed on top, one for each of the six weeks of Lent.

You will need:

a board about 2 1/2" wide and 1/2" thick cut into these lengths: one 16" length; one 12" length; two 4 1/2" lengths

sandpaper

paint or varnish (optional)

wood glue

glue gun

6 small clay pots, 2 1/4" diameter

one 6" PVC pipe, 1" diameter, cut into six 1" pieces

6 candles, all white; or 5 purple and 1 rose (be sure tapers fit inside the PVC pipe pieces)

paintbrushes

rose and purple craft paint

To prepare: Cut the board into the correct lengths and sand the pieces. If you'd like to further finish the wood, use paint or varnish and follow the instructions given with those substances. Let dry.

Using wood glue, attach the 12" piece horizontally on top of the vertical 16" piece, about 4" or 5" down from the top. Glue one of the 4 1/2" lengths under each end of the horizontal crossbar to stabilize. Let cross completely dry.

When your family is ready to complete the cross, cover your work area with newspaper or the like. First, paint the clay pots

inside and out (no need to paint the bottoms of the pots). Paint five with the purple paint and one with the rose color. Let all the pots dry well.

When the pots are dry, place a PVC pipe piece in the bottom of each pot and use the glue gun to secure it in place. These PVC pieces will hold the candles. Then glue each clay pot to the wooden cross following the pattern on the following page. Place the candles in the colored pots, pushing firmly into the PVC pipe pieces. If you chose colored candles, match the candle color to the pot color.

During Lent, light the candles each Sunday and on a daily basis, if you can. Use the lenten cross as the centerpiece for your dinner table, or display in another prominent place in your house.

On page 43, you will find some suggested prayers and readings which your family can use with the lenten cross. Feel free to develop your own rituals in conjunction with the cross. Just as the Advent wreath brings focus and spirituality to its season, the lenten cross can enhance and become a treasured part of your family's observance of Lent.

The blessing of the lenten cross found below can be said when you complete the cross, or use on Ash Wednesday as a way to begin the lenten season.

BLESSING FOR THE LENTEN CROSS

Dear God, we ask you to bless our cross. We pray that this symbol will help our family as we journey through Lent this year. May your presence strengthen us each day, filling our hearts with the joy of Jesus' resurrection, that all we say and do will be a reflection of your glory. Heavenly father, we pray that each of us might become a light for others during this holy season.

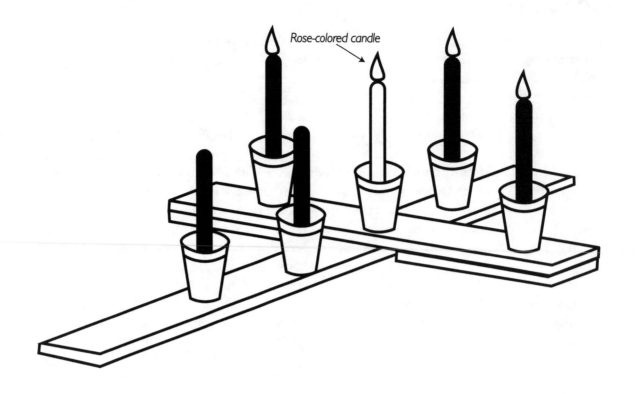

Rose-colored candle

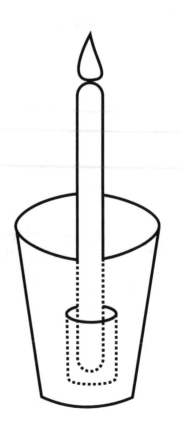

42

Prayers for the Lenten Cross

FIRST SUNDAY OF LENT

Theme: Strength

Light one purple candle

Scripture Reading: Matthew 4:1–11

Prayer: Lord, we pray for strength to resist the temptations that lead us away from you. Help us to follow your ways and open our hearts to your Word.

Discussion: Have each family member tell of a time when they resisted temptation.

SECOND SUNDAY OF LENT

Theme: Light

Light two purple candles

Scripture Reading: Matthew 5:14–16

Prayer: Dear Lord, let the light from these candles remind us that as your children, we are to be light for others. Let our actions and words be pleasing to you.

Discussion: What can you do this week to be a light to someone?

THIRD SUNDAY OF LENT

Theme: Peace

Light three purple candles

Scripture Reading: John 14:27–31

Prayer: Dear God, help us learn to share and compromise and practice peaceful resolutions to problems. We pray for all the people in the world who live in warring areas. Though danger surrounds them, may they know the peace that comes from believing in you.

Discussion: How might you peacefully handle your problems this week? Make it your goal to keep peace all week long.

FOURTH SUNDAY OF LENT

Theme: Joy

Light three purple candles and the rose candle

Scripture Reading: John 16:20–24

Prayer: Dear God in heaven, we rejoice that you are our loving father and teacher. Guide us and be with us in our efforts to be filled with joy in all we do at home, at school, at work, and at play.

Discussion: What makes you feel joyful?

FIFTH SUNDAY OF LENT

Theme: Forgiveness

Light four purple candles and the rose candle

Scripture Reading: Luke 6:27-36

Prayer: Heavenly father, you tell us to forgive others and love our enemies. Help us practice forgiveness here at home when we are angry or annoyed with each other. Fill us with your love and compassion that we might overcome our hurtful ways.

Discussion: Ask forgiveness of a family member you may have hurt this week. Talk about giving and receiving forgiveness. Share a hug of forgiveness.

SIXTH SUNDAY OF LENT (PALM SUNDAY)

Theme: Holy Week

Light all candles

Scripture Reading: Matthew 21:1–11

Prayer: Dear Lord, as we draw closer to Easter, let us be aware of your journey into Jerusalem; your washing of your disciples' feet and the Last Supper; your agony in the garden of Gethsemane; and your joyous resurrection on Easter morning.

As you gave your life out of your great love for all of us, let us give ourselves in love and service to others, that we might share in your resurrection and glory.

Discussion: What can you do as a family to journey with Christ through this Holy Week?

Flowered Cross

You will need:
- styrofoam cross (usually available at a craft store or florist)
- silk or plastic flowers with multiple blooms
- basket or bowl

This activity helps show how beauty and renewal can come from good works and sacrifice. Cut the multiple blossoms into individual flowers. Place these in the basket or bowl and set them near the cross.

Explain to your family that each time they do a good deed or kind act for another family member during Lent, they may place a flower on the cross. (The stems of the artificial flowers can be gently pushed into the styrofoam.) By Easter, you should have a beautiful cross covered in flowers to remind everyone how their little acts of kindness created a lovely decoration.

Habit Forming

You will need:
- letter-size paper
- pencil
- ruler
- crayons, colored pencils, or markers
- copy of an Easter picture

Make a copy of an Easter picture, one for each member of the family. You can copy the one on the next page, or find a picture in a religious book to trace, or draw your own picture using Easter symbols such as eggs, flowers, butterflies, rabbits, lambs, and the like. Grid the picture into 40 squares (If the paper is 8 1/2" x 11", make a 1/2" border in from all edges. Then measure five 1 1/2" squares vertically in from the border, and eight 1 1/4" squares horizontally in from the border.)

The night before Ash Wednesday, have each person choose one good habit they want to practice during Lent and write this on the back of their picture. Each evening of Lent, perhaps before or after dinner, talk about everyone's effort to practice their habit that day. If a person feels they practiced their good habit, they can color in one of the forty squares. If they had trouble that day, everyone could encourage them to try harder the next day. Then the following night, if that extra effort was made, the person could color in two squares. By Easter, the pictures will be transformed into a colorful representation of the good habits that were practiced.

44

Commemorating Holy Week

During this most solemn week of the liturgical year, join your family with Christians all over the world in remembering Jesus' passion and death.

The suggested symbols for each of the days can be used as a centerpiece for your table, or displayed in another part of your home where all will see them. The Scripture readings and discussion can be said as part of the evening meal—either before or after—or before bedtime.

SUNDAY (PALM SUNDAY)

Theme: We are people of praise
Symbol: Palms (use the ones from this weekend's liturgy)
Scripture Reading: John 12:12–13
Discussion: Each family member prays a prayer of praise to Jesus. Take turns praising each other, as well.

MONDAY

Theme: We are people of prayer
Symbol: Pretzels (the shape of a pretzel resembles arms folded in prayer)
Scripture Reading: Matthew 6:9–15
Discussion: Share thoughts on why it is important to pray, then compose a prayer together as a family.

TUESDAY

Theme: We are people of love
Symbol: Hearts
Scripture Reading: John 13:34–35, 15:9–11
Discussion: Let each family member decide how they can be more loving. Cut out and hang construction paper hearts throughout the house as a reminder to love better.

WEDNESDAY

Theme: We are people of forgiveness
Symbol: Rooster
Scripture Reading: John 13:36–38, 18:25–27
Discussion: Is there anyone in the family who needs forgiveness? Talk about how, even though Peter denied Jesus three times, he received God's forgiveness and went on to become the first leader of the church. As a family, ask forgiveness of God and of one another.

THURSDAY

Theme: We are people of service
Symbol: Water
Scripture Reading: John 13:3–14
Activity: Wash each other's feet or hands.

FRIDAY

Theme: We are people of obedience to God
Symbol: Cross
Scripture Reading: John 18–19:37
Discussion: Jesus was obedient even to death. Ask each family member to share their feelings about obedience.

SATURDAY

Theme: We are people of hope
Symbol: Rock (a reminder of the tomb)
Scripture Reading: John 19:41 and 42
Discussion: How do you think the disciples felt when they heard that Jesus was dead? Do we sometimes feel the same way? Why are we hopeful?
Activity: Make a Christ candle for Easter. Take a plain white candle, at least an inch in diameter. Decorate with Easter symbols, such as: eggs, lilies, butterflies, crosses, rabbits, and a sun. Cut shapes out of colored contact paper, then remove backing and stick on; or paint shapes on the candle with poster paints.

EASTER SUNDAY

Theme: We are resurrection people
Symbol: Christ candle (or any white candle)
Scripture Reading: John 20:1–18
Activity: Celebrate with a candlelight breakfast together. If you have colored Easter eggs, enjoy eating them as symbols of the resurrection.

OTHER ACTIVITIES FOR THE TRIDUUM

The triduum begins with the evening liturgy on Holy Thursday, and ends on Holy Saturday at the Easter Vigil.

• On Holy Thursday, set a small roll or piece of bread in the center of your dinner table, along with a special glass filled with wine or grape juice. Recall Jesus' words at the Last Supper—"Do this in memory of me"—and pass around the bread, having each person take off a small piece to eat. Do the same with the wine or juice.

• On Good Friday, take a small wooden cross, or use your lenten cross if you have made one, and give each family member a nail. In turn, have everyone pound their nail into the cross (parents, help your children with this!). If possible, keep silence in the house between 12:00 PM and 3:00 PM, to observe the time that Jesus hung on the cross.

• On Holy Saturday, make hot cross buns using the recipe on page 97 (or bake them ahead of time and freeze). Serve these for a special Easter breakfast.

• Attend the Easter Vigil or a sunrise service on Easter morning. (The Vigil usually lasts for at least two hours, so it may not be wise to take younger children.)

Triduum Centerpiece

You will need:

empty salt box with one end cut away,
    and 1/2" cut off one side from top to
    bottom
play dough (see recipe on page 92)
    or clay
a tray, or box with sides cut down
sand
real or plastic plants
a white cloth (a handkerchief is good)
large rock, to fit over cave opening
Jesus statue or doll, or a small crucifix

Cover an empty salt container with clay or play dough to give the illusion of a cave. (You can also fashion a cave out of papier mâché.) Place the cave, which represents the tomb, on a tray decorated with sand and desert plants. Set the tray in the center of your table.

On Good Friday, read one of the following Scripture passages: Matthew 26–27:61; Mark 14–15:47; Luke 22–23:56; or John 18–19:42. Take a figure of Jesus or a small crucifix, wrap it in a white cloth, and then place it in the tomb. (You could also use a small male doll to represent Jesus.) Put a large stone at the entrance of the tomb. Keep this *tableau* on your table through Holy Saturday.

Early on Easter morning, remove the stone from the cave and place the white cloth to the side. Take the Jesus figure out of the tomb and stand it in the sand, near the entrance. Keep the centerpiece on the table throughout the first week of Easter.

Stations of the Cross

You will need:

    list of the Stations of the Cross
    construction paper, poster board, clay,
       or play dough (see recipe on page 92)
    colored pencils, markers, or paints

You can begin this project early in Lent to have it ready for Holy Week or Good Friday. Using construction paper, poster board, clay, or play dough, fashion the Stations of the Cross. Divide into teams or work individually to do simple artwork illustrating the stations. You may want to use a Stations of the Cross booklet for ideas, or look at the stations in your church next time you are there.

When the stations are completed, set them up in one of the rooms of your home. (If weather permits, it's very effective to display the stations outside, whether on the porch or around your backyard.)

For a family Holy Week or Good Friday activity, walk from station to station, remembering how, through his passion and death, Jesus showed his great love for us.

THE STATIONS OF THE CROSS

1. Jesus is condemned to death
2. Jesus carries his cross
3. Jesus falls the first time
4. Jesus meets His mother
5. Simon of Cyrene helps Jesus to carry his cross
6. Veronica wipes the face of Jesus
7. Jesus falls the second time
8. Jesus meets the women of Jerusalem
9. Jesus falls the third time
10. Jesus is stripped of his garments
11. Jesus is nailed to the cross
12. Jesus dies on the cross
13. Jesus is taken down from the cross
14. Jesus is placed in the tomb

(Sometimes a fifteenth station—the resurrection—is added.)

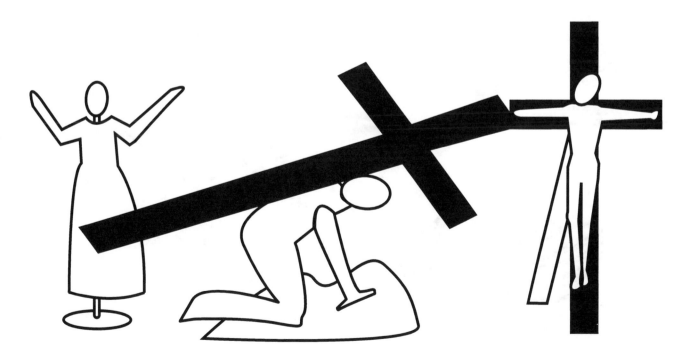

Easter Treasure Hunt

This Easter treasure hunt can be used instead of an egg hunt. (We usually have our hunt following church on Easter morning.) It uses biblical references to tell of the events leading up to the resurrection.

You can use our suggestions for clues, or make up your own. The items below go along with these clues, but be flexible and use whatever you have available and on hand. The children can take turns reading the various clues aloud (don't be afraid to step in if they get stuck on where to find some of the items.) As they are collected, place each item in an Easter basket.

You will need:
> clues for hunt
> a palm branch
> 30 nickels
> a small towel
> a kiss (press lipstick-covered lips to a piece of paper)
> small wreath (crown of thorns)
> a nail and small cross
> a lamb (stuffed animal or a picture)
> Bible with a bookmark to Isaiah 53

Ahead of time: Write out the clues, and hide the items throughout the house (or outside, if you prefer).

Clue One
> Hosanna! Hosanna! The people all cheered,
> When, riding on a donkey, Jesus appeared.

They covered his path with large leaves that were green;
So find a palm branch, then clue #2 will be seen.

Clue Two
> With thirty silver coins Judas was paid,
> In this way plans for Jesus' death were laid.
> You'll find these coins, and they number thirty,
> If you look in a place where the dishes are dirty.

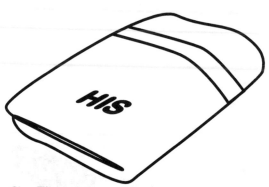

Clue Three
> At the Last Supper, Jesus acted in love.
> He washed his friends' feet in the room up above.
> He taught them to serve one another this way.
> Find your towel near something that tells time each day.

Clue Four

How Judas betrayed Jesus is hard to
    forget;
A kiss gave him away, now a kiss you
    must get.
Find yours on a paper in a special
    spot;
In wintertime, logs make this place
    very hot!

Clue Five

Jesus suffered for our sins,
But for our salvation he was born.
One of our plants holds the next thing
    to find—
You guessed it! a crown of thorns.

Clue Six

Jesus carried this up Calvary so our
    souls would not be lost.
They cruelly pounded his hands and
    feet; now find a nail and cross.
If you look very closely for the two
    things you seek,
You'll find them near an object that
    tells the days of the week.

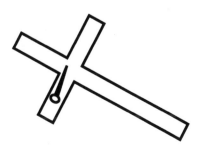

Clue Seven

As he hung on the cross—the Lamb of
    God, our Lord—
Jesus' side was pierced with a sword.
He died so we'd live forevermore.
Now look for a lamb in a kitchen drawer.

Clue Eight

The Scriptures foretold a great story
    you'll see,
That's found in Isaiah, chapter fifty-three.
It tells of a Messiah who would die for
    us all.
Find the Bible with this passage in a
    closet in the hall.

Clue Nine

The body of Jesus was laid in a tomb
It was cold and dark, a place of great
    gloom.
After three days, the women went to
    visit, in fear...
But an angel there told them, "He is no
    longer here!"
And this is the wonderful Easter Day
    news:
Jesus is alive! He is out of the tomb.

Jesus has risen and prepares us a place
Where we will live with him, and see
    him face-to-face.
As a sign of God's love, a small gift
    you will know
Waits in the living room. Hurry! 1...2...
    3...GO!!
(We usually leave the children's Easter
    baskets with small treats and pre-
    sents at the end of the hunt.)

Easter Doorknob Hangers

You will need:

    cardboard, poster board, or foam sheets
    scissors
    markers
    paint, glittery or plain
    glue
    stickers, sequins, other decorations

To begin, think of different messages your family can put on the doorknob hangers. Some ideas for the Easter season include: "Jesus is the light of the world"; "Alleluia, he is risen!" or "Lamb of God." Once several ideas have been written down, trace the doorknob hanger patterns found on the next page, and copy the pattern on cardboard or poster board or foam sheets. (Thin sheets of colored foam are usually available at a craft store, and are durable and easy to cut.)

Cut the hangers out and decorate them with words and pictures like the ones below, using the markers and/or paints. Stickers and other decorations can be glued on. If you are using foam sheets, use a hole punch to make holes in the scrap foam for a special "confetti" decoration. The little foam circles may then be glued on as decorations or borders.

If time permits, each family member can do more than one doorknob hanger. After the paint and/or glue have dried, everyone can hang their creations on doorknobs throughout the home. (Our children chose to hang theirs on their bedroom doors.)

Variation: These doorknob hangers are inexpensive and fun, and can be adapted to almost any season or time of celebration—Valentine's Day, Thanksgiving, Christmas, birthdays, and the like.

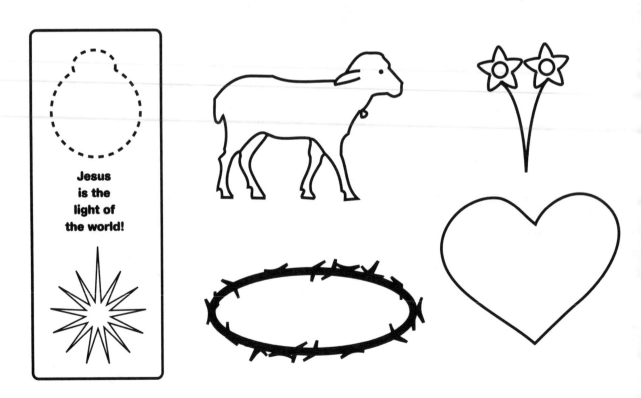

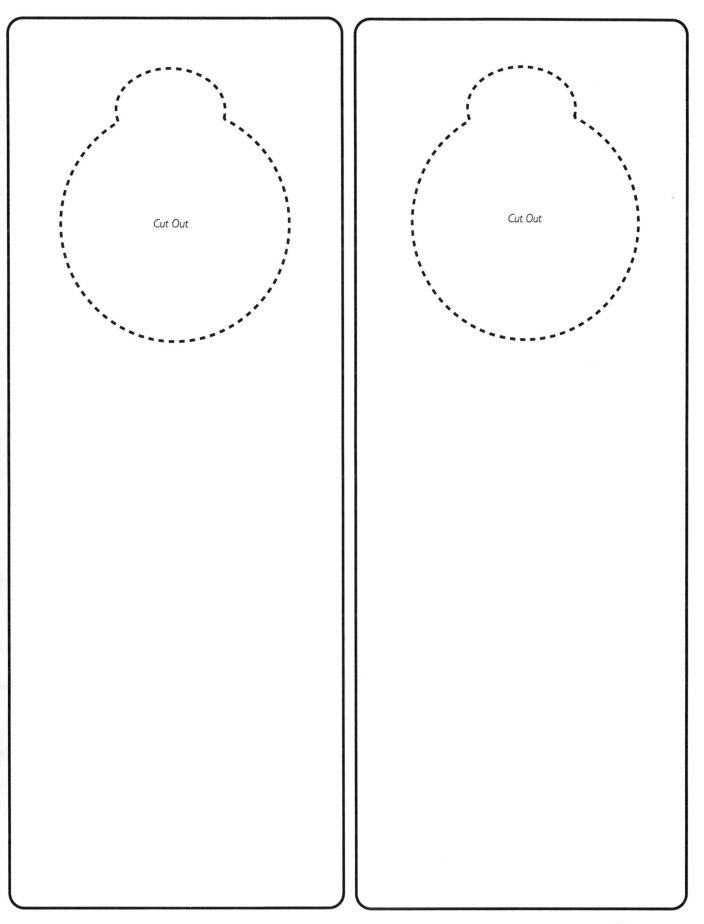

Cut Out

Cut Out

Lamb Piñata

This project might be done during Holy Week, and the piñata used on Easter day, after dinner. It takes at least a day to dry the papier mâché used to make the piñata, so plan accordingly.

You will need:

- one large round (oval) balloon
- one small round balloon
- two toilet paper rolls cut in half
    - or a paper towel roll, cut in fourths
- masking tape
- newspaper strips
- flour and water paste
- large bag cotton balls
    - or white and black paint
- black construction paper
- glue
- scissors or a small craft knife
- twine or heavy string

Blow up the two balloons and tie. Using masking tape, secure the balloons together to make the head and body of the lamb. Next, tape each of the paper rolls to a long side of the large balloon to form legs.

Now cover the body with papier mâché. (This process is messy, so prepare your work area accordingly!) To make a flour paste, take a cup or so of flour and slowly add water to it. The paste should be fairly thick, easy to work with but not runny. Rip newspaper pages into strips along the width of the paper. One at a time, take the newspaper strips and dip them thoroughly in the flour paste. Cover both balloons, as well as the legs, with several layers of newspaper, using the strips to strengthen

the bonds between the different parts of the lamb. Let dry for at least 24 hours.

When dry, glue on cotton balls to cover the entire piñata. Or, paint the lamb white, and make it look fluffy with curly black lines. Fashion ears, eyes, and a mouth with the construction paper, and glue these on. Make a tail out of cotton balls glued together, then fasten to the body of the lamb

Fill the piñata with toys and treats by cutting a small hole in the center top of the lamb. Form a large loop with the twine or heavy string, and secure it by taping to the inside of the top hole, then closing the hole back up. Suspend the piñata from a tree branch or a patio hook outside. **Caution: Do not play this game inside unless you have a large amount of space with nothing in the way that can get hit!**

To play the piñata game, have the children line up. In turn, blindfold each child and give him or her a broomstick or bat. Move the child near the piñata, then have him or her swing at the lamb and try to break it. (Make sure the other children are standing at a safe distance from the "swinger"!)

When the piñata is finally broken, the children scramble to pick up the candy and treats that fall out.

Variation: Use a large oval balloon to make an Easter egg piñata. Simply blow up the balloon, apply papier mâché as for the lamb, and let dry. Decorate with paints, string, or fabric trim. Fill with candy and treats, secure with a string for hanging, and play game as above.

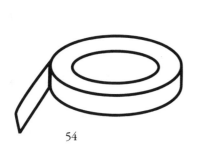   

Fancy Easter Eggs

Eggs are the ideal Easter symbol. Besides the obvious—new life springs forth from an egg—they can represent Jesus as he rose triumphant from the tomb. Here are a few variations on the traditional colored eggs.

TABLEAUX EGGS

You will need:

> blown-out eggs
> small scissors, such as manicure scissors
> clear or colored nail polish
> modeling clay
> little silk flowers and Easter figures
> Easter grass
> rick-rack or lace
> glue

To blow out the egg: Make a small hole with a needle or pin in the top of a raw egg. Make another hole, a bit larger, at the bottom of the egg. Now gently blow into the top of the egg, forcing the yolk and white out the bottom. (Make sure you have a dish ready to catch the insides of the egg!) Rinse out the inside of the egg, and let dry. This may take one or two tries to master, as it must be done very, very gently!

Using the scissors, carefully cut an oval about 1" in diameter into the side of the egg. (Decide whether you want your scene to go from the top to the bottom of the egg or horizontally, and cut accordingly.) Brush several coats of clear or colored nail polish on the outside of the eggshell to strengthen it.

Put a little modeling clay in the bottom of the egg, and gently place Easter figures, silk flowers, and whatever else you'd like into the clay. Place some Easter grass around the bottom of the figures to cover the remaining clay. Decorate around the opening with the rick-rack or lace. To stand the egg up, glue a small plastic ring to the bottom, or make a stand from a circle of cardboard stapled together.

TISSUE PAPER EGGS

You will need:

> hardboiled or blown-out eggs
> tissue paper, several colors
> liquid starch
> several small shallow dishes
> paint brushes

Tear up or cut the tissue paper into small pieces (like confetti). Put the tissue paper into a shallow dish; either mix the different colors together in one dish for a rainbow effect, or put each color in its own dish.

Pour some of the liquid starch into another shallow dish. Using a paint brush, coat an egg with liquid starch and roll it in the pieces of tissue paper. Let dry. Display the finished eggs in a basket or clear bowl.

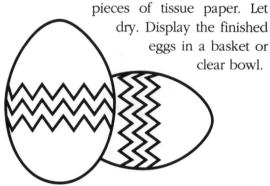

EGGSHELL MOSAIC

You will need:

> dyed eggshells
> plastic bags (sandwich size)
> poster board
> coloring book picture (optional)
> glue

Save the eggshells from your hardboiled dyed Easter eggs, separating them by color into the plastic bags. When you are ready to use them, carefully crush the shells in the plastic bags. Draw a simple picture on the poster board or glue a page from a coloring book on poster board. "Color" the picture by gluing on the crushed colored eggshell pieces.

Pentecost Windsock

The feast of Pentecost falls on the seventh Sunday after Easter, and marks the close of the Easter season. Wear red to church on Pentecost, and serve red foods for dinner and/or dessert.

You will need:

Bible
lightweight poster board (bright color)
construction paper
scissors
crêpe paper for streamers
stapler or tape
hole punch
yarn or string

To begin this activity, read a Scripture passage about Pentecost to the family. (We suggest John 14:25–26, John 16:13, and Galatians 5:22.) Talk about several objects that are used as symbols of the Holy Spirit (eg., flames for tongues of fire, a dove, a heart, clouds for wind, as in the illustration below}. Cut a few of these symbols out of construction paper. Next, cut the poster board in half width-wise, and attach the symbols. You can also add appropriate words or other designs, if you'd like.

Staple or tape the two long sides of the poster board together to form a circular windsock. Staple or tape several crêpe paper streamers around the bottom of the tube. Punch four evenly-spaced holes near the top of the windsock. Attach equal pieces of yarn or string to each hole, then bring these together and tie in a knot at the top. Hang your family's windsock outside to remind you of the spirit of Pentecost.

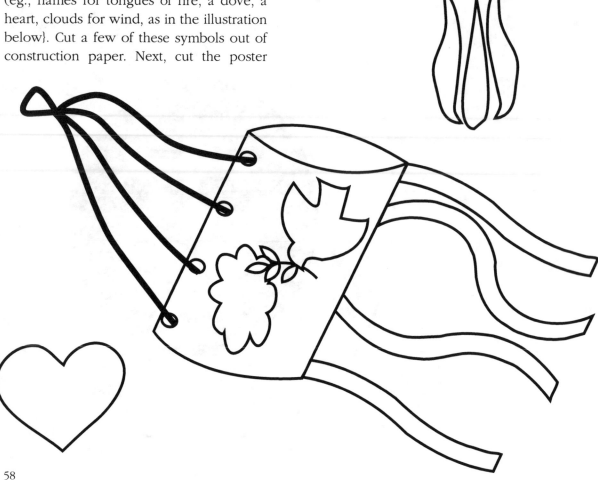

CHAPTER FIVE

Celebrations All Year Long

This chapter offers a variety of seasonal ideas to enrich existing holidays, as well as some favorite ways to observe birthdays, anniversaries, and sacrament celebrations.

Year-Round Tree

You will need:

    tree branch
    spray paint (optional)
    coffee can or a large clay or plastic pot
    fabric scraps or contact paper
    glue (for fabric)
    paint and brushes (for clay)
    several small rocks or plaster of paris
    various decorations, purchased or made

If you want to paint your branch (you can also leave it "natural"), take it outdoors, spread plenty of newspapers under the branch, and spray paint. While the paint is drying, decorate the coffee can or plastic pot with fabric scraps and glue or contact paper. If you want to use and decorate a clay pot, tempera paints work best.

To make your tree, place the tree branch in the coffee can or pot, anchoring it with several rocks or "cementing" it in with the plaster of paris. (Follow the directions given on the plaster of paris.) When the branch is secured, put it in a prominent spot in your home, and decorate for the occasion you will be celebrating.

The year-round tree is a fun ongoing project. You can hang orange pumpkins with black yarn at Halloween; paper eggs and crosses at Easter; and miniature flags for the Fourth of July. At the beginning of school, use little red apples, numbers and letters, pencils, and erasers to decorate the tree. During Advent, the branch can be used as a Jesse tree. On birthdays, find or make ornaments that reflect the birthday person's likes and interests.

Each month your family can redo the tree to reflect the celebrations taking place during that month. Be on the lookout all year long for new little items to add to the tree. If it's in your budget, shop right after each holiday when ornaments and lights go on sale.

Variations:

•Use a small artificial Christmas tree instead of a branch, or try a small live potted pine.

•Between celebrations, hang each family member's rosary on the branches.

Secret Valentines

You will need:

Bible

small, heart-shaped pillow or decorated cardboard heart

Note: You could make a heart pillow or a decorated cardboard heart as a family time project.

At dinner or during a family time on February 1, bring out the heart pillow or decorated heart and explain that it is a "Secret Valentine." Then read Matthew 6:1–4 to your family.

Have one member of the family start the secret Valentine on its way by secretly doing something nice for someone else in the family. He or she then leaves the heart nearby. For example, Mom can make someone's bed and then tuck the heart beside the bed pillow. When that person sees the heart, he or she in turn does something nice for someone else without their knowing, and leaves the heart nearby.

Continue doing this each day until February 14. Use the heart at dinner that evening for a centerpiece, and share some of the nice things that family members have done for one another.

Candy Kisses

Make your own kisses to give to family and friends on Valentine's Day!

You will need:

16-ounce package of almond bark

2/3 cup peanut butter

12-ounce package semi-sweet chocolate chips

foil

several greased funnels (aluminum or plastic)

paper strips

6-8 cups crisped rice cereal

Melt the almond bark according to package directions. In a separate pan, melt the chocolate chips and stir in the peanut butter. Add the chocolate mixture to the almond bark. Stir in the cereal. Press this mixture into funnels that have been lightly greased with butter or shortening, then place the funnels on a cookie sheet in the refrigerator to harden.

Once the mixture is set, carefully remove from the funnels and wrap in aluminum foil. Have the family write messages on the paper strips and stick into the "kisses."

Love Bags

You will need:
- lunch bags (white ones work best)
- scissors
- pink plastic wrap or red construction paper
- tape and glue
- construction paper, stickers, markers

Trace a heart shape on the front of each bag, and cut this heart out. Place a rectangle of the pink plastic wrap or construction paper on the inside of the bag over the heart opening, and tape in place inside the bag so that the color shows through the cutout. Decorate the outside of the bag with construction paper hearts, markers, stickers, and the like, adding one or two Valentine messages, as well.

Use the bags as a special treat for lunches on Valentine's Day. Or you can fill a few bags with candy or cookie treats, and share them with teachers, neighbors, and friends.

MOTHER'S DAY & FATHER'S DAY

Candy Card

You will need:
- several different candy bars and candy
- poster board or large sheet of paper

Make a candy card for Mom or Dad (older children or the other parent can help younger children with this project). Buy several different kinds of candy and candy bars. Using your creativity, write appropriate sentiments which incorporate the candy names on a poster board. For example: "Dear Dad: Don't SNICKER, but we think you are the best dad in all the MILKY WAY. You are a LIFESAVER to our family and worth more than $100,000." Tape the candy bars to the poster board in place of the candy names.

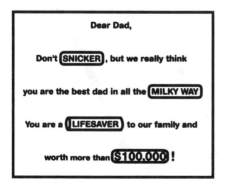

Dear Dad,

Don't SNICKER , but we really think

you are the best dad in all the MILKY WAY

You are a LIFESAVER to our family and

worth more than $100,000 !

Variation: Make a card for Mom or Dad on letter-sized white paper or construction paper, with a greeting that uses the names of candy and candy bars. On Mother's or Father's Day, have the children present the appropriate candy bar as the card is read aloud to Mom or Dad.

Other Activities

•Take the family on a Mother's Day picnic. Make sure that Mom is totally "off the hook" as far as any food preparations go! Have Dad and children make picnic food, or pick up some take-out food along the way. Spend a leisurely afternoon letting the children play and the parents truly relax. (If Dad is the main cook in your house, give him the same "break" on Father's Day.)

•Decorate your year-round tree on Mother's and Father's Day with notes of appreciation, representations of Mom or Dad's interests or hobbies, and other appropriate items. If you are giving any presents, wrap and place by the tree.

Patriotic Placemats

You will need:

- 8 1/2" by 11" red and blue construction paper, one sheet of each color per person
- 11" by 14" pieces of white paper, one sheet for each person
- scissors
- glue or clear tape
- clear contact paper

Cut the red and blue paper into strips, 1" wide by 11" long. Fold the white pieces of construction paper in half, width-wise. Cut a straight line from the fold to within 1" of each outside edge. Continue doing this down the page, making the slits 1" apart.

Open up the mat, then begin alternately weaving in the red and blue strips from bottom to top along the short side of the white paper. Take a red (blue) strip, and weave under and then over the white portions towards the top. Then take a blue (red) strip and weave opposite of the first strip, over then under. Continue alternating this way. (For weaving diagram, see Stained Glass Window on page 11.) Keep the colored strips close to each other while you weave. When you have woven in a few strips, it may be helpful to secure the ends of the woven strips down with a small dab of glue or a piece of tape.

When the placemat is woven, cover with clear contact paper and use for meals on the Fourth of July. (You can use these place-mats on other national holidays, as well.)

Streamers

You will need:

- paper towel tubes, covered with white paper or white poster board cut and stapled to form a tube
- large marker (black, red, or blue)
- red, white, and blue crêpe paper, cut into strips about 1' long
- scissors
- glue, tape, or a stapler

If you are using a paper towel tube, cover it with white paper and secure with glue, tape, or staples. Using a marker, write on the tube "USA: One nation under God, indivisible, with liberty and justice for all!" or another patriotic slogan.

Attach red, white, and blue crêpe paper to one end of the tube. The streamers can then be hung like a windsock (attach a long piece of string to the inside of the tube, forming a loop for hanging), or tape a dowel to the inside of the tube and use the streamer as a "flag" as the children march in a mini-parade.

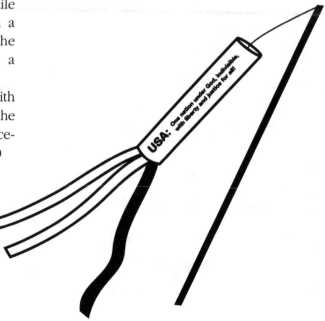

Fireworks Flags

You will need:

    black construction paper
    glue
    glitter
    dowel or stick

Use glue to "draw" fireworks shapes on the black paper, then sprinkle glitter on the wet glue. When the glue has dried, attach the construction paper to a dowel or some other type of stick so that the "flag" can be carried in a parade.

Other Activities for the Fourth

•Make banners out of red, white, and blue fabric that feature patriotic slogans. These can be used in a parade or hung from porches and front doors.

•A Fourth of July parade is a good opportunity for neighbors to get to know each other, so why not organize a mini-parade for your block and the blocks surrounding it? Make invitations to the parade and deliver them to all the homes in your neighborhood. Encourage the children to decorate their bikes, wagons, skateboards, and scooters to use in the parade. Children (or parents) who play an instrument can provide marching music. (Drums and drummers are usually in good supply among young children!)

    Following the parade, a potluck dessert or meal could take place in someone's backyard.

HALLOWEEN

Giving Ghost

You will need:
    copies of the Giving Ghost letter
    treats

About the third week in October, reproduce two copies of the Giving Ghost picture and the Giving Ghost letter. Make or buy two sets of treats to go along with the letter and the ghost picture. Secretly deliver the treats, letter, and Giving Ghost to two neighbors on your street or block.

We first tried this activity a few years back, and wondered if the idea would even make it past the first two houses. But what a surprise: within a week, we saw Giving Ghosts on many of the doorways in our neighborhood! And by the end of October, the Giving Ghost had made its way back to our own houses.

This is a great activity for neighborhood community-building.

GIVING GHOST LETTER

Unless you want your house to be haunted this year, you must take treats to two homes on this street. You have only one day to comply, so hurry!

Post this Giving Ghost picture on the outside of your front door. Keep it there until Halloween. It will keep all other ghosts away. Make two copies of this letter and the picture. Deliver them with treats to two homes that don't have the Giving Ghost posted.

These treats can be used for the Giving Ghost, or make up a few batches for Halloween trick or treat-ers.

Ghost Pops

You will need:
    white almond bark
    chocolate chips
    popsicle sticks
    wax paper or foil
    cookie sheets
    plastic wrap
    orange and black ribbon

Melt the almond bark according to package directions. (You can substitute baker's semi-sweet white chocolate for the bark, if you'd like.) Cover the cookie sheets with wax paper or foil and place the popsicle sticks about four inches apart on the sheets. Spoon or carefully pour the melted almond bark in a ghost shape over the top of each stick. Use the chocolate chips to make eyes. Refrigerate until firm.

When solid, wrap each pop in clear plastic wrap, and tie with orange and black ribbons.

Mini Jack-o'-Lanterns

You will need:
    oranges
    whole cloves or magic markers

Decorate oranges with markers or whole cloves to make jack-o'-lanterns. These also make good treats to give with the Giving Ghost.

Giving Ghost

Thanksgiving Banner

You will need:

a piece of brown felt or fabric for banner, about 18" by 36"

several pieces of fabric or felt in various fall colors

needle and thread or sewing machine

scissors

glue or glue gun

dowel and string for hanging

small basket or box

Start this project at a family time in early November so that you have plenty of time to complete the banner by Thanksgiving.

Sew or glue a casing along the top of the banner to fit in the dowel. Cut out letters from the other colors of felt or fabric to spell: "Now Thank We All Our God, with…" (use the letter patterns found on pages 101–103, or make your own). Glue the letters to the background, across the top.

Cut out a few hearts, a pair of hands (trace a child's hand for a pattern), and a few notes (or the word "VOICES") from different colors of fabric. Also cut out fruit shapes and a cornucopia using the patterns on the following pages. Glue the hearts, hands, and notes underneath the letters. Beneath these three items, place the cor-

nucopia, leaving enough room on the banner to add fruit as the days go by. Put the fruit shapes in a basket or box kept close at hand.

As you work, talk with your family about how we show our thanks to God by doing loving deeds (hearts) and by helping others (hands), as well as with kind words and joyful singing (voices). When the banner is complete (this may take more than one family time to finish), hang it in a prominent place.

During the time before Thanksgiving, encourage everyone to show their gratitude for God's goodness with kind words, loving deeds, and helping hands. Each time a good action is done, take a fruit from the basket or box and attach it to the banner, near the cornucopia. By Thanksgiving, your cornucopia should be spilling our with the "fruits" of your family's thankfulness and good works.

Variation: Instead of cutting out letters and symbols from fabric, use various colors of fabric paint to draw these on the banner. The fruit shapes can also be made from construction or colored paper. If you do choose fabric for your letters, etc., you can use iron-on backing to attach the pieces to the banner.

Thankful Turkey

You will need:
  poster board
  large turkey made from construction
    paper or drawn and colored with
    markers on the poster board
  large construction paper feathers in
    different colors
  tape

Make a large turkey without tail feathers out of construction paper to fit the poster board; or draw and color one with markers on the poster board. Cut at least twenty feathers out of different colors of construction paper, enough to make a full tail for the turkey.

About three weeks before Thanksgiving, have the children start taking turns adding a feather to the turkey. On each feather the child writes something he or she is thankful for. By Thanksgiving, the turkey's tail should be filled with lots of feathers—and lots of thankfulness!

Thank-You Notes

You will need:
  paper
  pencils, markers, or crayons

Spend one of your November family times making "I'm thankful for you because…" notes to give to teachers, grandparents, family members, neighbors, and friends at Thanksgiving. Young children can color pictures to give.

You might also do this for members of your parish who you would like to recognize, or staff at the school. Another nice touch would be to make some of these cards for a local nursing home or hospital.

Sing Thanks

You will need:
  Bible
  hymnal or religious songbook

Read Ephesians 5:19–20 aloud to your family. Find a few Thanksgiving hymns such as "Now Thank We All Our God" and "Praise God from Whom All Blessings Flow." Reflect together on the past year, and mention some of the things that you are grateful for as a family. Sing the Thanksgiving songs together as a sign of gratitude for God's blessings.

Bouquet of Thanks

You will need:

6 wooden skewers

clay pot, about a 4" diameter at top

54" long green ribbon (1/4" wide), cut into six 9" pieces

construction paper in various colors

small piece of styrofoam to fit into the bottom of the clay pot

glue or glue gun

different colors of tempera paint

small rectangles of kitchen sponge, no bigger than 1" around

paper plate

spanish moss (available in craft stores)

raffia or calico material for a bow

At the start of your family time, have everyone list several things—twice as many items as you will have flowers—for which they are thankful. Save this list to refer to later.

Cut out flowers using the patterns below, or create some of your own; make six flowers in all. Make doubles of each flower. Using the list you wrote up earlier, write one thing that your family is grateful for on one side of each flower. Then match up the two copies of each flower, and with the writing sides out, glue the pieces together with a skewer in between. Do this with all of the flowers. Press firmly and set aside. Push the piece of styrofoam into the bottom of the pot. Glue it in place if it seems loose.

Pour a small amount of each of the paint colors onto the paper plate, each in a separate area. Using a different sponge piece for each color, take turns lightly dipping the sponge into the paint and then applying it to the clay pot. (The sponge pieces can be blotted on a rag or paper towel if too much paint adheres after dipping.) Sponge-paint the whole pot and then set it aside to dry.

Tie a piece of the green ribbon into a bow on the skewer under each flower. When the pot has dried, stick the flowers into the styrofoam. Arrange the "moss" in the pot around the skewers to hide the styrofoam.

Using a scrap piece of calico or some raffia, tie a bow and glue it to the front of your pot. You now have a beautiful centerpiece to grace your dining room table for the month of November.

I am grateful
for my books

71

Birthday Crown

This crown has an adjustable velcro fastener so that it can be used for many years. Make one crown for the entire family to use alternately on each birthday; or make individual crowns for each child.

You will need:

> poster board or cardboard
> 2 pieces of 24" by 8" felt or fabric (use gold or a favorite color of the birthday child)
> glue or glue gun
> needle and thread (optional)
> sequins, fake jewels, fabric paint
> 4" strip of velcro
> 24" strip of rick-rack (optional)

Using the pattern found on page 36 or creating your own design, cut out a crown from the poster or cardboard. Then, cut two matching crowns from the gold fabric. (Make sure that the ends of the crown are long enough to fit around a child's head, with a generous amount left for fastening and for growth.)

Trim the cardboard crown 1/8" all the way around. Cover the cardboard with the fabric pieces and sew or glue around the edges. Attach rick-rack trim along the bottom of the crown. Attach the velcro pieces to the ends of the crown. Use sequins, fake jewels, and fabric paint to decorate.

Our birthday crowns have lasted for many years. The crown is presented to the special child bright and early on the morning of his or her birthday, along with a chorus of "Happy Birthday."

Birthday Banner

You will need:

> fabric or felt for the background
> glue or glue gun
> needle and thread (optional)
> fabric scraps, paints, other decorations
> dowel and string for hanging

Sew or glue a casing at the top of the banner. Cut out the letters of the child's name, and fasten these along the middle of the banner. (The child's name can also be painted on with fabric paints.) The first year, make a few symbols that represent events or interests in the child's life: hobbies, sports, awards, sacraments, and the like are a good place to start. Use appliques, iron-on pieces, patches, or make your own symbols from fabric or paper.

Each year, add a new item to the banner that reflects something special or important that has happened that year in the child's life. Include the birthday person in deciding on the new symbol for that year, or keep it a surprise and have the rest of the family brainstorm and suggest ideas.

Present the banner to the child, along with the birthday crown, on the morning of his or her birthday. If you have a video camera, have someone pan (move the camera over) the banner, capturing all the past symbols as the child looks over his or her special banner. Display the banner in a prominent place in your home during the day, then either put the banner away until next year or hang it in the child's room throughout the year.

Other Birthday Activities

•On each child's birthday, take time during the day to look through his or her personal photo album or a family album that shows him or her from babyhood on. You can also look through baby books, calendars, and other memorabilia from the child's early years.

•In place of a purchased card, make a collage of words and pictures, cut out from newspapers and magazines, that describe the birthday person. The family can glue their contributions to a poster board or a large sheet of sturdy paper. Cover the card with clear contact paper to help preserve it.

•Send the birthday person to bed shortly after dinner on the eve of his or her birthday. (Perhaps he or she can have a new magazine or book to read during this time.) The rest of the family then sets to work preparing for the birthday. Bake and decorate the cake, string streamers, decorate the birthday child's chair at the table, wrap and put out presents. Early the next morning, everyone comes into the birthday child's room to wake him or her up with a song. The child is then led to see the special preparations the family did in their honor.

•Take out the birthday child's baptismal candle, secure it in a candleholder, and display in a prominent place. These candles can be purchased at a religious goods store if you don't have the original candle. Light the candle at the birthday meal, and spend a few minutes talking about what it means to be baptized.

You might prefer to do this on the anniversary of each family member's baptism. If the child was named after a particular saint, look up some information about the saint and share it with the family at mealtime.

ANNIVERSARIES

Wedding anniversaries are very important. After all, a marriage is the beginning of a family. Here are some ways to celebrate this very special time:

•Parents can make up a crossword puzzle using clues that relate to the time of their early courtship, their wedding, and first years together. Give your children the puzzle and see how many clues they can fill in. Children may learn a lot about their parents that they didn't know.

Or make up a word search such as the one below. Parents can make a list of several words about themselves and their wedding day. These words are then hidden vertically, horizontally, or diagonally in a letter grid. (It may help to use graph paper for this project.) Give your children a list of the words that you've hidden, and ask them to draw a ring around the words as they locate them.

•Have a special dessert on the day that matches your wedding date each month. For instance, if you were married on June 23rd, then on the 23rd of each month, you would have the same special dessert—e.g., angel food cake, oatmeal cookies, or chocolate cupcakes—to commemorate the occasion. On your real anniversary, your family could decide on a new "anniversary dessert" for the following year.

•Each year, on your actual anniversary, take out your wedding album or show the video from your wedding. If that's not possible, describe the ceremony to your children, mentioning where the ceremony and the reception took place, who was there, what you ate, where your honeymoon was, and the like.

•On your next wedding anniversary, do indeed go out as a couple. But let the children join in the celebration, either before or after the actual date, by serving anniversary cake and ice cream to mark the beginning of your own special family.

Sample Word Search

Answers can be found on page 100.

```
G  N  I  C  N  A  D  A  L  E  P  A
N  D  C  O  I  R  D  Y  O  J  S  R
I  G  R  O  E  S  A  N  V  M  R  E
R  P  A  Y  M  J  U  L  E  K  A  C
A  G  R  O  O  M  T  M  P  Y  E  E
C  T  E  R  P  O  I  P  I  E  S  P
I  L  Y  T  G  I  F  T  S  G  R  T
M  O  A  E  N  E  D  I  M  N  G  I
S  V  R  O  I  R  S  T  J  E  T  O
T  R  P  B  R  I  D  E  O  Y  N  N
M  P  A  R  O  V  E  T  S  U  R  T
```

List of words to find:

CARING	BRIDE
PRAYER	GROOM
JOY	LOVE
DANCING	COMMITMENT
RECEPTION	TRUST
GIFTS	RING
CAKE	MUSIC

Table Runner
for First Eucharist

You will need:

plain fabric to make the runner, long
enough to fit the length of your table
trim for edges, if desired
fabric paints
appliques (optional)

Using a fairly heavy fabric, cut a runner to fit your table. Turn under a small hem on all edges, and decorate the edges with rick-rack, lace, or another trim, if you wish. In the middle of the runner, use the fabric paints to write your child's name and the date of his or her first Eucharist. Decorate the runner with appliques and other designs made with the paints.

At the child's celebration party, have family members and friends sign the cloth with the fabric paint. They can also add short messages. On each anniversary of your child's first Eucharist, use the runner on your dinner table to serve as a reminder of this special occasion.

Variation: Prepare the banner in secret, having family and friends sign the banner without the recipient knowing. This makes a lovely surprise gift.

Celebration Plate
& Blessing Cup

The celebration plate and blessing cup can be used as part of special holiday meals, at birthdays or anniversaries, when someone gets good grades or a promotion, when your teen gets a first job, if someone needs cheering, or to honor a visitor.

Choose a special plate—use a family heirloom, buy a plate at a religious goods shop or card store, or find an unusual plate at a yard sale or discount store. Do the same with a wine or water goblet.

Set the celebration plate at the place of the person who has a special occasion to mark. At the beginning of the birthday meal, fill the goblet with grape juice and pass it around the table. Each family member takes a sip, tells why the person being honored is special to them, then passes the cup along to the next person.

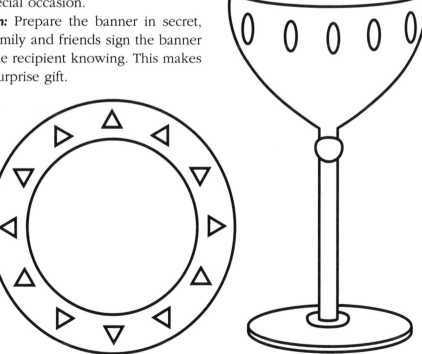

"Vanilla" Times

Not every day can be a holiday. The reality is that routine, "vanilla" days exist, but they can still be occasions for fun family times. While the activities in this chapter aren't exclusively religious, they do provide opportunities for families to share time and be together.

Balloon Burst

You will need:
   a few sheets of white paper
   pens or pencils
   scissors
   balloons
   a bulletin board
   paper strips
   thumbtacks
   darts

Have everyone cut the white paper into strips, then write down one fun activity on each strip. For example: have a family hug, eat a treat, play a board game of your choice, tell one thing that you like about every other family member, or sing a song.

Place these strips inside the balloons, one in each. Blow up balloons, tie the ends, and fasten them to the bulletin board with the thumbtacks. Lean the board against a wall, and take turns trying to pop the balloons with a dart, starting with the youngest family member. (It may be best to play this outside!) When someone pops a balloon, everyone stops and does the activity written on the strip.

If you don't have access to a bulletin board and/or darts, or are concerned about safety, have everyone sit on the balloons to pop them.

Variation: Instead of jotting down activities on the strips of paper, write down various Scripture passages for the family to find in a Bible and read aloud.

Bingo

You will need:
   a bingo game
   small prizes (optional)

If you choose to have small prizes, wrap at least one for each player. When someone gets a BINGO, he or she chooses one of the prizes but doesn't unwrap it. When the next person wins, he or she can take the prize from the first winner or choose a new prize. If someone wins more than once, he or she can trade prizes, but can only keep one prize. As soon as everyone has a prize, they can be unwrapped.

Variation: Have a "charity bingo." Ask everyone to donate a handful of pennies (about fifty-cents worth). Use the pennies to cover the BINGO spots as the numbers are called out. After each game, put the pennies that have been used as markers into a pot or jar. At the end of your family time bingo, the pennies can be donated to a chosen charity.

Word Search

You will need:
> several sheets of graph paper or paper with grid lines drawn on
> pencils
> word list

Divide your family into two teams. Each one will design their own word search to challenge the other team. Choose a topic for both teams to use: some ideas include holiday words (the sample below uses a Christmas theme), Bible story words, Jesus' miracles, or vacation spots.

First, have each team make a list of words for the topic. Then, create a word search with all the words on each team's list included horizontally, vertically, diagonally, or even backwards. Other letters are filled in to help hide the key words.

When each team is done with their grid, they give it to the other team along with the list of words to find. Each team circles the words as they find them. If you want to add an extra challenge, set a timer for five minutes or so and see which team can find all their words before the timer rings.

Variation: Design a word search using the letters from a Scrabble game. Circle the words with yarn when they are found.

Answers can be found on page 100.

Sample Word Search

```
C H R I S T M A S
S Q T R A E P N H
H T R R A T S A S
T N E S E R P T T
A L E R S N O I R
E C M I V C P V O
R I R L K T O I K
W H P I S M T T C
C A N D L E S Y S
L G X R P Q R T R
```

List of words to find:

CHRISTMAS

PRESENT

WREATH

CANDLE

STOCKING

NATIVITY

TREE

STAR

The Category Game

You will need:
> cardboard cut into small 2" or 3"
>   squares, about 20 cards altogether
> markers or crayons

On each card, write a category name such as flowers, cities, clothing, food, girl's names, or states. Shuffle these cards and place face down. The first person chooses an alphabet letter to start the game and says it aloud. Next, that person turns over the top category card. Each player, starting with the person to the left of the choosing person, must try to name something in that category that starts with the selected letter.

For example, if the person chose the letter "B" and turned over the "food" category card, each person would have to name foods that start with the letter "B," such as butter, beans, bananas, or bagels. When a person cannot think of an item, they may pass. When everyone is stumped, a new letter is chosen as well as a new category.

Variation: Make a Bible category game using categories such as saints, biblical locations, Old Testament figures, New Testament figures, books of the Bible, or things mentioned in the Bible.

Thgin Sdrawkcab

You will need:
> various items for relays

Have everyone put their clothes on backwards (or inside out) for this family time activity. If you start this family time with lunch or dinner, have a small dessert first, then the main course.

Choose any of the relays below, or make up a few of your own. For each of these games, divide into two teams.

1. Pouring relay: Each person must use the opposite hand from the one they normally use to pour beans from a plastic pitcher into 3 empty cups. Try not to spill any!

2. Writing relay: Set up a chalkboard or large piece of paper at one end of a room. Each team member must run from the opposite end of the room to the board or paper and write "Backwards Family Time" backwards, then run back into place.

3. Shoulder toss: Drop clothespins over your shoulder into a bucket placed behind you.

5. Spelling bee: Have a spelling bee which uses simple words. The only catch is that the words must be spelled backwards.

6. Toe-tac-tic: Everyone gets a partner and plays tic-tac-toe in reverse. Any player with a complete line of "X's" or "O's" loses.

If you have access to a video camera, have someone take a video of your activities. Play the video, then show it in reverse!

Silly Stories

You will need:

several different short stories—simple and familiar tales such as "The Three Little Pig" or "Little Red Riding Hood" work well

(if you type up the stories, double-space the lines for writing room)

Divide into two teams. Give one of the stories to the first team, and have them quietly read through it. Above several key words mark what part of speech they are: nouns, verbs, adjectives, adverbs, or proper nouns. (With nouns, you may want to specify name, place, or thing.) The team may want to go into another room to do this part, as it usually involves some discussion.

When the first team has finished this step, they ask the other team to supply words to replace those that are marked in the story *without* reading the story to them. For example, if the first word marked is a noun, the second team would be asked to name any noun. The first team would then write down the noun given in place of the original noun.

When all the marked words have been replaced, one person on the first team reads the story aloud to the others. Give a new story to the second team, and begin the process again. **Note**: Even if your children are too young to know what nouns, adjectives, etc., are, they learn quickly which kind of word you are searching for.

Variation: Make up your own stories with blanks to fill in.

KEY: N = noun   PN = proper noun   ADJ = adjective   VB = verb

Once upon a _____ (N), there was a family of _____ (Plural N) who lived in a

_____ (ADJ) cottage deep in the forest. There was a great big _____ (N), a medium-

sized _____ (N), and a tiny little _____ (N). One spring morning, the _____ (Plural N)

had prepared some _____ (ADJ) _____ (N) for their breakfast. But as the _____ (N)

was too _____ (ADJ) to eat, they decided to go for a _____ (N) in the woods while

it cooled. They had only gone a short while when along came a little _____ (N)

named _____ (PN). She was picking wild _____ (Plural N) in the field next to the big woods.

She saw the three bears' cottage. "Oh, how _____ (ADJ)!" Goldilocks said to herself,

"I wonder who _____ (VB) there?"

Nobody was home, so she opened the _____ (N) and went right in. She saw

a table with three bowls of _____ (N) on it, and feeling hungry she _____ (VB) the

porridge in the great big bowl. "Ouch! This is too _____ (ADJ)." Then she tasted the

porridge in the medium-sized bowl. "Oh! This is too_____ (ADJ)!" Then she _____ (VB)

the _____ (N) in the tiny little bowl. "Mmmm. This _____ (N) is just right!" And

she ate it all up.

Goldilocks was feeling tired. Seeing _____ chairs, she decided to sit down
                                        Number
for a bit. She_____ into the great big chair that belonged to Papa Bear. "Oh!
              VB
This chair is much too _____!" She tried _____'s chair. "Humph, this one is
                        ADJ   PN
much too _____." She went over to the tiny little_____ that belonged to
          ADJ   N
Baby Bear. "This one looks just right." But do you know what happened as soon as

she _____ down on it? Crack! The little _____ broke!
     VB   N

       Goldilocks got up. She _____ the stairs to the bedroom. Yawning, she pulled
                               VB
down the _____ and got into Papa Bear's great big _____. But it was too
          N   N
hard. She climbed into Mama Bear's medium-sized _____. But that was too soft!
                                                  N
Then she climbed into Baby Bear's tiny little _____ which was just right. And
                                               N
Goldilocks fell fast asleep.

       Just at that moment, the _____ bears returned from their walk , feeling
                                 ADJ
very hungry indeed. All they could think about was the tasty _____ waiting for
                                                              N
them on the table. "What's this!" said Papa Bear in his great _____ voice.
                                                               ADJ
"_____ has been _____ my porridge!" "Oh my," said Mama Bear, in her
  PN   VB ending with -ING
medium-sized voice. "Someone has been eating my _____ !" "Oh no!" cried
                                                  N
Baby Bear, in his tiny little voice. "Someone has been _____ my porridge and
                                                        VB ending with -ING
they've eaten it all up!"

       Then Papa Bear said, in his great big _____ . "Why, someone has been
                                              N
_____ in my chair!" "And someone has been sitting in my _____ !" said
VB ending with -ING   N
Mama Bear, in her medium-sized voice. And Baby Bear cried, in his tiny little voice,

"_____ has been sitting in my _____ , and now it's broken!"
  PN   N
       Then the _____ bears climbed up the _____ to the bedroom.
                 ADJ   N
"Someone has been _____ in my bed!" cried Papa Bear, in his great big voice.
                   VB ending with -ING
"_____ has been sleeping in my _____ !" said Mama Bear in her medium-
  PN   N
sized voice. "Someone has been sleeping in my bed!" cried Baby Bear, in his tiny little

voice "AND HERE SHE IS NOW!"

Name That Sound

You will need:

   a tape recorder and blank tape
   paper and pencils

Divide into two teams. Send one team on a scouting mission, while the other team goes off into another room with the door closed. The scouting team must make a tape recording of several different sounds. These can be from inside or outside the house. (The other team can play a simple game like Tic-tac-toe or Old Maid while they are waiting.)

When the first team has recorded 6 to 8 sounds, they come back and play the tape for the other team. That team has to guess what each sound is. When they are done, trade places and let the second team go scouting for sounds.

Sing Along

Gather the family together, and sit in a circle. To start, have someone sing the first line of a popular song or hymn, and then point to someone else. That person must try to sing the next line of the song, then choose someone to sing the third line.

This can be done in teams, also. You might want to allow a certain number of "passes" to be used when a player cannot remember a line.

Variation: Try doing this with familiar poems instead of songs.

Fiction-ary

You will need:

   paper strips and pencils
   dictionary

Give everyone several strips of paper, about ten or so each, and a pencil. One person—he or she can be called the "chooser"—finds a word in the dictionary and asks if anyone knows the meaning of that word. If no one can define it, the word is "playable." Each person then makes up a definition of the word trying to make it sound as authentic as possible. Have everyone write down their definition on a strip of paper, initial it, and hand it in to the chooser. (The chooser must write down the actual definition on his or her strip of paper.)

When everyone has handed in a definition, mix the strips up and read each one aloud. Each person has one vote to choose what they believe is the real definition of the word. After the voting is done, the correct meaning is read. The person to the right of the chooser becomes the new chooser, and play continues as before.

If younger children are playing this game, you might want to pair them up with an older child or an adult.

pul·chri·tu·di·nous (pŭl′krĭ-tood′n-es) *adj.*

82

Scavenger Hunt

You will need:
- 2 identical lists of items
- a timer
- 2 bags or pillowcases

Before you begin this family time activity, have someone go through your house or backyard (or both) and make a list of clues for items that can be found relatively easily. There should be at least two items for all clues on the list, so that each team can find something for the full list.

Divide the family into two teams and give each team the same list of items to find and a bag or pillowcase to put the items in. Set the timer for whatever seems reasonable. The teams set out to find as many items on their list as possible before the timer rings. When time is up, the two teams can empty out their bags and compare what they have gathered.

You can use the list given here for your scavenger hunt, or prepare your own.

SCAVENGER HUNT LIST

Find something that...
- is money
- tells time
- measures
- is soft
- holds things together
- is blue
- helps you think about God
- has wheels
- is fuzzy
- rings
- uses numbers
- goes on your foot
- relates to music
- makes your family happy
- is square-shaped
- is round

Spring Flowers

You will need:

    various colors of tissue paper, 20" by 26"
    scissors
    pipe cleaners

To make each flower, cut five rectangles of tissue paper, approximately 5" by 13"; these can be cut from one color paper, or mix and match the colors as you wish. Stack the five rectangles, then fold them back and forth in fan fashion along the long edge (the folds should be about 1/2" across). For scalloped edges on the flowers, round the two ends of the "fan" with the scissors.

Secure the middle of the tissue-paper fan with a pipe cleaner and twist to hold. Then spread out the fan and fluff up each layer to the center to create a flower look. Put all the flowers in a vase or basket, and use as a bouquet to celebrate the first day of Spring, May Day, or Mother's Day.

If your family has an altar for Mary during the month of May, you could display a bouquet of these flowers there. You might want to make the flowers in various shades of blue tissue paper as a Marian tribute.

"Write On"

You will need:

    scrap paper
    pencils
    8 1/2" by 11" sheet of white paper

Design a set of family stationery or thank-you notes. (For our own families, we chose to make thank-you postcards.) Have everyone sketch out ideas, using favorite symbols, pictures, or words that represent your family. Look at each person's idea, and try to include part of all the ideas into one drawing for your stationery or card.

When you've come up with something that everyone (or almost everyone!) agrees on, make a clean copy of the design on a piece of 8 1/2" by 11" paper. (If you are doing a postcard or notecard, you can draw to the size you want or have the copy shop reduce the design to the correct size.) Take the design to a copy shop and have them duplicate as many pieces of stationery or cards as you'd like, at least enough to give everyone in the family a few sheets for their own use.

Children can use the stationery or notes for writing thank-you's at Christmas and birthdays. If time and finances permit, you may want to have each child design his or her own thank-you cards or personal stationery. In addition to providing a ready supply of writing material, having one's own stationery is great for self-esteem.

Family T-Shirts

You will need:

T-shirts, one for each person
aprons or old shirts
newspapers
various colors of fabric paints (one different color for each family member)
paper plates or pie tins

Have everyone pick out one clean T-shirt, or purchase new ones for this project. (We usually buy boy's or men's undershirts, which are reasonably priced.)

"Paint proof" your workers and work area with the aprons or old shirts and newspapers. Pour some paint onto the paper plates or pie tins, one color per plate. Have each family member choose one of the colors for themselves. Lay out the T-shirts on the covered work area.

Each family member dips one hand in his or her chosen color and then handprints each shirt with that color. For example, Dad dips his hand in green paint and then prints his hand on his own shirt and the rest of the shirts, each time using the green paint.

When completed, each shirt should contain the same number of handprints as there are family members. If desired, you can paint each person's name on their shirt. Or, you can paint a family slogan across the back of each shirt, such as, "I'm a member of the Thompson family!" or "Hooray for the O'Hara's!"

Chalk Mural

You will need:

paper for planning
colored chalk

As a family, plan a mural on paper that you can then draw on your driveway or sidewalk. This might reflect an upcoming holiday or season, or use a scene from a Bible story (e.g., Noah's ark and the rainbow or Moses and the burning bush). You may want to copy a picture from a book or magazine as a guide.

Once the picture is planned, go outside and make an outline on the driveway or a sidewalk to work within. Draw the mural and then let everyone color it in with the chalk.

Variation: Have each family member lie down on the sidewalk, and trace around him or her. Then fill in the self-portraits with the chalk.

And the Nominee Is...

This ongoing family activity encourages everyone to be on the lookout for good works and kind words within the family.

You will need:

several sheets of plain paper
scissors
pencils
a basket

Type or write up a sheet of paper, like the example shown, with this or a similar nomination message:

```
I nominate _____
for "Notable Person of the Week"
because_____.
    Signed,_____
- - - - - - - - - - - - - - - - - - - - - - - - -
I nominate _____
for "Notable Person of the Week"
because_____.
    Signed,_____
- - - - - - - - - - - - - - - - - - - - - - - - -
I nominate _____
for "Notable Person of the Week"
because_____.
    Signed,_____
```

Make several copies of the sheet, then cut up the strips of paper and place them into a basket along with a pencil or two. Put the basket somewhere that it can be easily reached.

When one family member notices another being extra helpful or nice during the day, he or she can nominate the other by filling out a strip of paper. At the end of the day (we do this right before dinner), read and acknowledge, perhaps with applause, all the nominations that have been placed in the basket that day.

Once a week, draw one slip out of the basket. The person who was nominated on that slip wins a small prize such as an allowance bonus, or gets to choose a fun activity.

Tangrams

You will need:

poster board, cardboard, or floor tile
    that can be cut with scissors
ruler
pencil
scissors

Trace the tangram pattern shown on the next page onto the poster board, cardboard, or floor tile. Cut the pieces out. Now gather the family together, and have everyone try to make different pictures with the tangram pieces. (You may want to make a set of tangrams for each family member.)

The tangram pieces can be used to make many different designs, but you must always follow two rules to make the pictures:

1. All seven pieces must be used for each picture.

2. Each piece should touch at least one other piece, but no two pieces can overlap.

Some ideas are shown here to get you started. See how many different pictures the whole family can make. If each person has their own tangram set, try using all the sets to make a family picture.

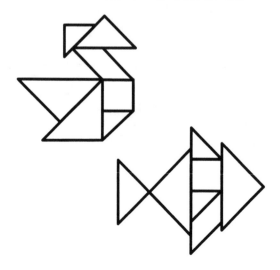

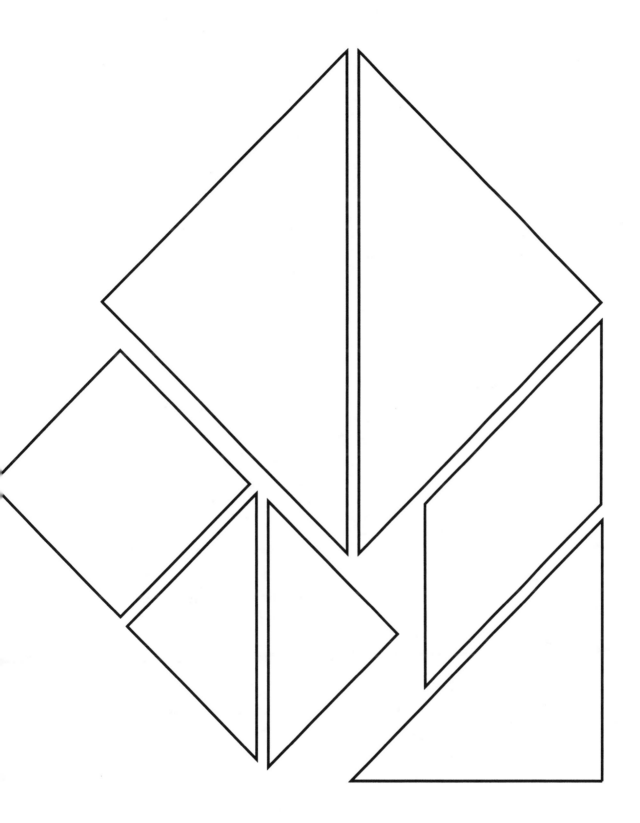

Summer Book Worm

This project is an excellent way to stress the importance of reading. Get everyone involved by listing all the books that they read during the summer.

You will need:
> butcher paper or poster board
> markers or tempera paints
> ruler
> a black marker

On butcher paper, draw and color a large worm with a smiling face. (You can use the picture on the facing page as a guide.) With the black marker, draw about fifty lines up and down the worm's body. (If you use paint for coloring the worm, make sure it is dry before you draw in the lines!)

Have everyone in the family write down the name of each book they read during the summer as they finish reading it. Perhaps a few minutes of your weekly family time could be taken to record the books that have been read during the previous week.

You can also use some family time to read aloud together at least once a week, maybe every night, if possible. (Fifteen minutes a night is a good start for a family reading session.) Encourage older children to read aloud to the rest of the family. They may even enjoy giving dramatic readings or using interesting voices for the characters in a particular book.

Here follows a list of suggested books for reading aloud. These are also good for individual reading, too; most are on an intermediate reading level. Many of them are classic children's stories which have well stood the test of time. Also, check with your local library for their recommendations on new releases.

The Incredible Journey, by Sheila Burnford.

The Boxcar Children, by Gertrude Chandler Warner. *There are many excellent books in this series.*

Anne of Green Gables, by L. M. Montgomery. *Also read the sequels to this book.*

My Friend Flicka, by Mary O'Hara

Little Pilgrim's Progress, by Helen L. Taylor.

The Secret Garden, by Frances Hodgson Burnett.

Charlie and The Chocolate Factory, by Roald Dahl. *Also look for other books by Dahl, including* **James and the Giant Peach**.

The Reluctant Dragon, by Kenneth Grahame.

Little House on the Prairie, by Laura Ingalls Wilder. *This is another series of books worth reading aloud.*

The Man Called Magic, by Paul Gallico.

The Black Stallion, by Walter Farley. *There are several books in this series.*

Misty of Chincoteague, by Marguerite Henry.

Charlotte's Web, by E. B. White.

The Indian in the Cupboard, by Lynn Reid Banks. *Try the other books in this series, too.*

Treasure Island, by Robert Louis Stevenson.

1. _____
2. _____
3. _____
4. _____

5. _____
6. _____
7. _____
8. _____

Helping Hands Chart

You will need:
- large poster board for chart
- colored paper for children's hands and job strips
- two fabric squares, 2" or 3" around
- pencils and markers
- glue or glue gun
- paper clips
- decorative stickers

Trace each child's hand on the colored paper, write his or her name on the hand with a marker, and cut the hands out. Take the fabric squares: on one write "regular jobs," and on the other write "special jobs." Along the left side of the poster board, glue down the two fabric squares on three sides of the fabric, leaving the top edge open to form a pocket. Glue the children's hands along the top edge of the poster.

Make two lists, one of chores that need to be done on a regular basis (setting the table, washing dishes, dusting, laundry), and those that are done infrequently (weeding the yard, cleaning the basement or garage, washing the car). Cut the lists into individual strips, with one job on each strip. Put the jobs in the appropriate pockets on the poster ("regular" or "special").

Each week, have each child take three jobs from the regular pocket and one from the special pocket, and attach them to his or her "hand" with paper clips. At the end of that week, the children get a sticker under their names on the poster for each job that was successfully done. Then take all the completed jobs from that week, put them back in the right pocket, and have everyone choose another set of jobs.

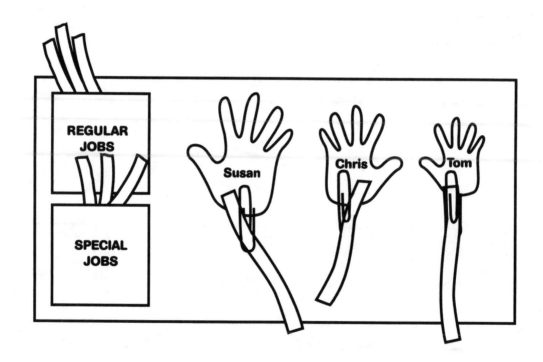

Summertime Activities

•On the last day of school, start a tradition of doing something special. Have a picnic in the park, go out for ice cream, or have a small shopping spree (this could even have a practical clothes-for-summer theme).

•In a large manila envelope or a used giftbox, one for each child, save important school papers, awards, souvenirs from outings, photos, greeting cards, letters, and other memorabilia from the school year.

•Hold a family campout in your backyard. Pick a warm, clear night, and get out the sleeping bags (don't forget flashlights!). Gaze at the stars, roast marshmallows on the barbeque grill, and tell ghost stories.

•Try to arrange for Mom and Dad to spend some time alone with each child during the summer. Some activities can be a dessert night out or a breakfast out, an early morning or afternoon bike ride, a hike in the woods or a long walk, a game of basketball or tennis. Leave time for conversation, especially if your children are older.

•Start a Friday night movie and popcorn tradition. Rent a video which the whole family can watch together, or go out to a movie. Cook up some popcorn (mix in M&Ms for a special treat), or have another favorite family snack.

•Before the first day of school, write a letter to each child encouraging them to do well during the year. Include a few coupons such as "Good for one bed-making"; "Good for making one lunch"; "Good for a ride to school." These can be "cashed in" on those days when a child might be running behind.

CHAPTER SEVEN

Someone's In the Kitchen...

The kitchen is a great place to share family time and fun together. Below you'll find directions for making play dough; the rest of this chapter has recipes for just plain eating!

Homemade Play Dough

You will need:

    2 cups flour
    1 cup salt
    2 cups water
    2 tablespoons vegetable oil
    1 package unsweetened kool-aid
    4 teaspoons cream of tartar
    wax paper

Mix all the ingredients in a pan. Cook over low heat until the dough starts to stick. Remove to wax paper and let cool about fifteen minutes. Form into a ball and store in an airtight container.

Use this dough for some of the projects found in the previous chapters, like the figures for the Stations of the Cross or Christmas ornaments. You can sculpt it or make shapes with cookie cutters. And don't overlook the therapeutic value of simply working with play dough. Many of the minor frustrations of the day seem to melt away as you poke and pound the clay!

Marshmallow Rainbow

You will need:

    wax paper or paper plates
    colored mini-marshmallows
    peanut butter or honey
    knife or other spreader
    Bible

Together with your family, read aloud the story of Noah's ark (Genesis 6–9:17). Talk about the meaning of promises and covenants, and ask everyone to remember a time when someone promised them something. Was the promise kept? How did each person feel when it was—or wasn't?

Now, give everyone a piece of wax paper or a large paper plate. Spread either the peanut butter or honey in a half circle. Then stick on the marshmallows to form a rainbow—one color for each line of the rainbow.

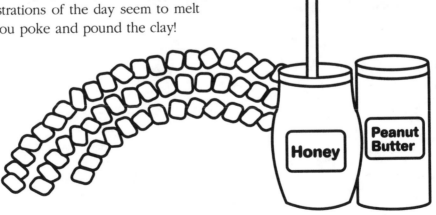

Sugar Cookies

This dough needs to be refrigerated before being used for cookies.

You will need:
  1 cup shortening, softened
  1 1/2 cups white sugar
  2 eggs
  2 tablespoons milk
  2 teaspoons vanilla
  2 1/2 cups flour
  1/2 teaspoon salt
  1/2 teaspoon baking powder
  cookie sheets
  cookie cutters
  colored sugars or frosting

Mix the shortening, sugar, and eggs together, then add the milk and vanilla. Stir in the dry ingredients and chill the dough well (at least four hours or overnight).

When you are ready to make the cookies, preheat the oven to 400 degrees. Work with about one-fourth of the dough at a time, keeping the rest refrigerated. Roll out a portion on a floured surface. Cut with cookie cutters and sprinkle with colored sugars before baking. (The cookies may be left plain and frosted afterwards, too.) Place the cookies on a lightly greased cookie sheet, and bake for five to seven minutes.

We make these sugar cookies at Christmas and Valentine's Day each year using cutters appropriate to the holiday. The cookies freeze well if put into tightly sealed containers.

Variation: Create "sports cookies" for the sports enthusiasts in your family. Fashion basketballs, soccer balls, or baseballs with a round cookie cutter. Tint some frosting orange for the basketball background and use white for the other balls. Using an empty mustard or ketchup squeeze bottle filled with chocolate frosting, add the details to the balls.

Quick Cookies

You will need:
  12-ounce package chocolate chips
  4 cups cereal
  6 tablespoons peanut butter
  wax paper
  cookie sheet

Melt the chocolate chips and the peanut butter in a pan on the stove or in the microwave. Stir in 4 cups of a cereal of your choice (try one that's not heavily sweetened, like cheerios or rice krispies). Drop this mixture by teaspoonfuls onto a cookie sheet covered with wax paper. Refrigerate a few minutes to harden and then eat!

Neighborhood Cookie Plate

You will need:
  plate
  baked treat
  written note

Bake some cookies or brownies or a cake—you can also purchase these—and place them on a special plate. Include a note similar to the following:

"Please enjoy these treats. We think you are special neighbors. When the plate is empty, please refill it with a treat of your choice and send the plate and a note on to your next-door neighbors."

Together with your family, bring the plate over to your next-door neighbor's house. The first time we tried this activity, we weren't sure whether we would ever see our plate again. How pleasantly surprised we were a month or so later when the original plate was returned to us filled with cookies! It had circled our entire block.

Ice Cream Sandwiches

You will need:

    1/2 gallon of ice cream, packed in a
        rectangular carton
    one egg
    one chocolate cake mix
    1/2 cup shortening
    1/4 cup softened margarine
    1 teaspoon vanilla

Heat the oven to 375 degrees. Beat the egg, shortening, margarine, vanilla, and half the cake mix until smooth. Stir in the other half of the cake mix.

Divide this dough into 4 equal parts. Roll each part into a 10" by 6" rectangle on a lightly-floured surface. Cut each of these rectangles into 8 smaller ones and lift carefully onto an ungreased cookie sheet. Bake five to six minutes, and remove cookie sheet from oven. Immediately, lightly prick each piece with a fork several times and let cool.

When the cake pieces are completely cooled, take out the ice cream and open from one side. Slice off a block of the ice cream, and cut into pieces that fit in between two of the cake pieces. Continue making the rest of the ice cream sandwiches in this way. Wrap any that aren't eaten in plastic wrap and freeze. This makes 16 sandwiches.

Try different flavors of cake mix and ice cream to vary this treat.

Ice Cream Cake

You will need:

    an angel food cake or lady fingers
    small plastic containers with lids (small,
        soft margarine tubs are a good size),
        one for each family member
    ice cream, sherbet, or frozen yogurt
        (use several different flavors, if
        desired)
    chocolate syrup (optional)

Soften the ice cream, sherbet, or frozen yogurt. Give each person a large piece of cake or several lady fingers, which they then tear into small pieces and place in their plastic container.

Next, stir in the ice cream, sherbet, or yogurt. If you'd like, drizzle some chocolate syrup over the top of the "cake," then put the lid on the container and freeze for half an hour. The "cake" is then ready to eat.

Orange Swirl

This recipe serves two to three people, and is perfect for a hot summer day!

You will need:

    4–5 ice cubes
    2–3 scoops vanilla ice cream
    1/2 cup milk
    blender
    1 teaspoon vanilla
    1 cup orange juice

Mix all the ingredients in a blender until smooth, then pour and drink.

Microwave Fudge

You will need:

3 cups chocolate chips
1 can condensed milk
1/3 cup powdered sugar
2 teaspoons vanilla

Grease an eight" square pan or a bread pan. In a glass bowl, microwave the chips and milk on high for two minutes. Stir. Add sugar and vanilla and stir well. Pour into the greased pan and refrigerate for at least four hours.

Ice Cream Cone Cupcakes

You will need:

9-ounce package cake mix
1 egg
6 tablespoons water
12 plain cake-type ice cream cones
frosting and sprinkles

Mix the cake mix and egg, then add the water. Beat until smooth. Fill the ice cream cones half-full with batter and set in a microwave muffin tin or in glass custard cups arranged in a circle.

Microwave on medium (50% power) for 2–3 minutes or until a toothpick inserted in the center of the cupcake comes out clean. **Note:** You can only bake six cupcakes at a time. Remove baked cones to a cooling rack and repeat with the other six cones. These may be frosted and decorated with sprinkles when cool.

Popping Out

Making popcorn together can be part of a discussion on how God's great love brings changes into our lives.

You will need:

vegetable oil
1/2 cup popcorn kernels
pot or 12" skillet, with cover
salt, butter, other seasonings to taste

Read the following passage aloud: "So if anyone is in Christ, there is a new creation: everything old has passed away; see, everything has become new" (2 Corinthians 5:17).

Show the children the popcorn kernels, and ask if they know how these hard, dry kernels become the fluffy white popcorn we like to eat. Explain that inside each kernel is a tiny bit of moisture. When the kernels are heated, this moisture turns into steam and explodes, causing the kernels to burst into popcorn.

You can then relate how choosing to be Christian is like making popcorn. When we recognize God's great love for us, enormous changes happen inside our hearts. We become filled with God's love; in turn, that love bursts out toward others in caring, giving ways.

Wrap up this family time by making popcorn together, the old-fashioned way. Put 2 tablespoons of vegetable oil in a large pot or skillet, then drop in 3 kernels only of the popcorn. Cover the pot and turn the burner on to medium-high. Listen carefully for the pops—the oil is hot enough when all 3 kernels have popped.

A parent or older child should then carefully pour in the rest of the kernels. Replace the cover and shake the pot back and forth across the burner until the popping is done. Remove from the heat; add salt and butter or other seasonings such as grated parmesan cheese and pepper.

The recipes on the next two pages are especially appropriate for the lenten season.

Coated Pretzels

You will need:

    a bag of pretzels for eating (whatever
        size your family enjoys)
    almond bark or semi-sweet chocolate
        squares
    wax paper
    cookie sheet

Tell your family the legend of how pretzels came about (see "The Story of Pretzels"). Next, melt the almond bark or chocolate squares according to package directions. Dip the pretzels in the melted candy, and use tongs to remove them. Place the dipped pretzels on wax paper on a cookie sheet and let them harden for a few minutes in the refrigerator.

While you are dipping the pretzels and letting them cool, talk about prayer. You can lead off a discussion with questions such as:

- What is prayer?
- How do you know when someone is praying?
- Where do we pray?
- What are some times we pray?
- What are some prayers we know?
- Can you remember some times that Jesus prayed?

Before sharing your pretzel treat, recite this simple prayer:

Our arms we fold, our heads we bow;
For food and drink we thank you now.

Variation: Instead of dipping pretzels, open a tube of uncooked breadsticks and shape the sticks into a pretzel. Place these on a cookie sheet and sprinkle sea salt or kosher salt over the tops. Bake according to directions on breadstick package.

The Story of Pretzels

Long, long ago, when knights lived in castles, girls and boys were eating pretzels. Drawings of pretzels can be seen on a sixth-century manuscript in the Vatican library in Rome, which means that pretzels may have been around for fourteen-hundred years!

You may wonder how pretzels got their unusual shape. Most people believe a folktale about a certain monk who set out to bake some bread for Lent. (Because people in early times could not eat milk or eggs during Lent, this dough consisted of flour, water, and salt.) The monk didn't want to waste any dough left after forming his loaves, so he rolled the dough out into thin strips. Then he took these strips, put one end over the other, twisted them, and pressed the ends to the top of each loop.

To the monk, the shape looked like children's arms folded in prayer. (In those days, people often prayed by folding their arms across their chests.) He called the twists of dough "bracchiola," a Latin word meaning "little arms." Over the years the name eventually became "pretzels."

The monk then went about giving his pretzels to the poor people of his town to use for food during Lent. Today we enjoy this snack at any time of the year. But pretzels can be a special lenten reminder of our call as Christians to take care of the poor and needy people in our world.

Hot Cross Buns

This recipe makes 24 hot cross buns and 24 plain buns. You can also double the amounts of raisins, citron, and nutmeg listed below and stir into all the dough to make 48 hot cross buns.

You will need:

1 package active dry yeast
1 1/2 cups warm water (105 to 115 degrees)
1 cup unseasoned lukewarm mashed potatoes
6 to 7 cups all-purpose flour
2/3 cup shortening
2 eggs
1 1/2 teaspoons salt
2/3 cup sugar
3/4 cup raisins
1/4 teaspoon ground nutmeg
1/3 cup chopped citron
1 egg white, slightly beaten

Dissolve the yeast in warm water in a large bowl. Stir in the potatoes, sugar, shortening, eggs, salt, and 3 cups of the flour. Beat until smooth. Mix in enough remaining flour to make the dough easy to handle. Turn dough onto a lightly floured surface; knead until smooth and elastic, about 5 minutes. Place in a greased bowl; turn greased side of dough up. Cover bowl tightly, and refrigerate at least 8 hours but no longer than 5 days.

When you are ready to make the buns, take the dough from the refrigerator and punch it down. Divide the dough in half. Cut one half into 24 equal pieces, shaping each piece into a ball. Place about 2 inches apart on greased cookie sheet. Cover and let rise until double.

Squeeze raisins, citron, and nutmeg into the other half of the dough. Cut into 24 equal pieces. Shape each piece into a ball; place about 2 inches apart on greased cookie sheet. Cut a deep cross into the top of each ball with a sharp knife. Cover and let rise until double, about one hour.

Heat the oven to 375 degrees. Before baking, brush the tops of buns with egg white. Bake until golden brown, about 20 minutes. When cool, frost crosses on tops of buns with Quick Frosting (recipe below) or ready-made frosting from a tub.

Quick Frosting

3/4 cup powdered sugar
2 teaspoons water or milk
1/4 teaspoon vanilla

Mix the ingredients together until the frosting is smooth and of spreading consistency. Use a knife or small spatula to spread.

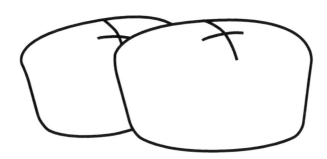

Other Kitchen Activities

•Make it a priority to bring the family together at dinner for a time of sharing and reconnecting. Consider unplugging the phone or turning on the answering machine while your family is eating. This may seem like a radical step at first, but you will most likely discover that uninterrupted mealtimes allow more pleasant and relaxed conversation and family sharing to take place.

•To provide a sense of continuity and security, you might try to eat dinner together at approximately the same time each evening, although afterschool activities and parents' work schedules make this a challenging goal. Plan crockpot, microwave, or easy-to-fix meals for busy nights; enlist the help of your children in food preparation whenever possible.

•One family we know has an "open-door" policy for dinner. This means that the parents or their nine children always feel free to invite a guest for dinner. Possibly the salad is made bigger or another loaf of bread is sliced; but family members and friends alike are all honored and made to feel at home and welcome. (This can be a great way to encourage teens to stay around and enjoy dinner!)

•If you don't have the space at your home for entertaining, why not invite another family to join your family at a nearby park? You may want to have a picnic, as frugal or extravagant as you wish. Paper plates, and plastic utensils and cups minimize cleanup, and the park provides entertainment for the children.

•One night for dinner, near the end of the school year, make a double recipe of a casserole. Use one dish for your own family, and put the other dish aside to deliver to a favorite teacher as an end-of-the-year gift. You can also do this for each of your children's teachers or for the school staff or the principal, if time and resources allow.

•During each trip to the grocery store, pick up an extra item: canned goods, a box of macaroni, household products, and the like. Put these aside, and donate them on a regular basis to a pantry or homeless shelter in your community.

ACROSS

1. A devotion to Mary
2. Feast of the 3 kings
3. Our Creator
4. Jesus is the _____ of the world
5. What God has for everyone
6. A blessing with oil
7. Laws God gave us
8. Giving honor to God
9. Area guided by bishop
10. Talking to God
11. Presides over a diocese
12. Messenger of God in the Old Testament
13. Jesus' foster father
14. Third person of the Trinity

DOWN

7. Our religion
10. The apostle who denied Jesus 3 times
15. Jesus' mother
16. Son of God
17. God's winged messenger
18. Mary's angel
19. God's kingdom
20. Loving care or forgiveness
21. Boy who challenges Goliath
22. Holy Communion
23. A calling from God
24. Outward signs instituted by Christ to give grace
25. Jesus' 12 special disciples
26. Jesus was raised here

Sample Word Search

List of words to find:

CARING	BRIDE
PRAYER	GROOM
JOY	LOVE
DANCING	COMMITMENT
RECEPTION	TRUST
GIFTS	RING
CAKE	MUSIC

Sample Word Search

List of words to find:

CHRISTMAS

PRESENT

WREATH

CANDLE

STOCKING

NATIVITY

TREE

STAR

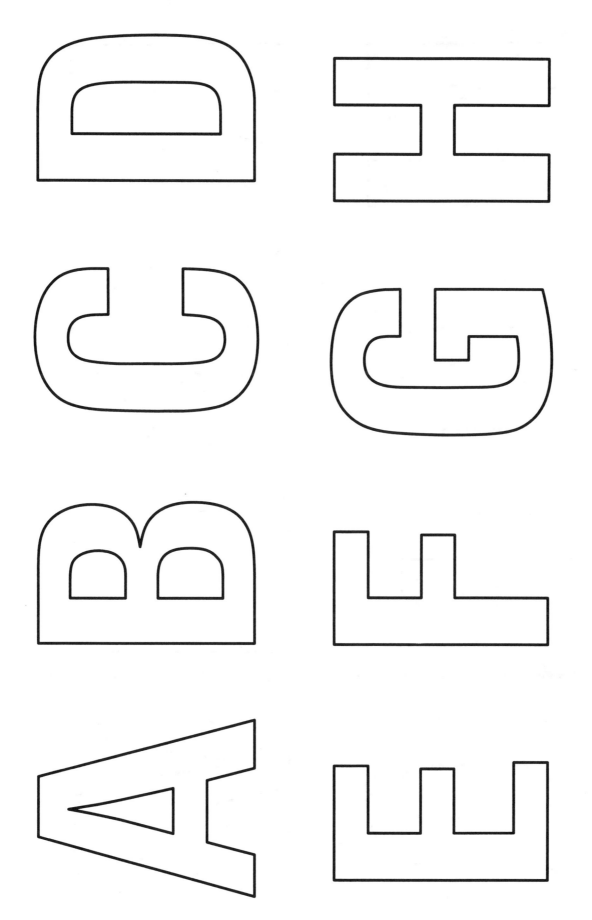

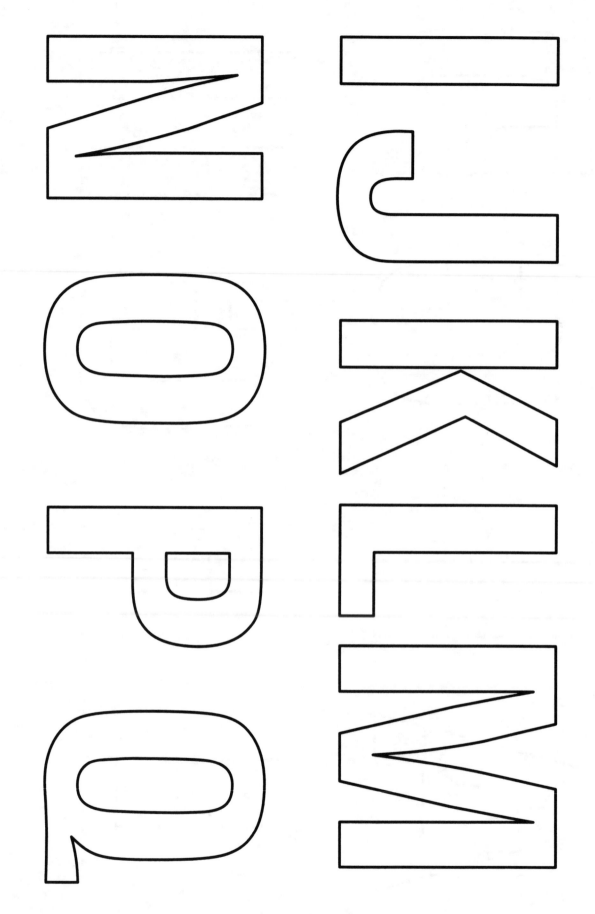

103

Of Related Interest...

Family Prayer for Family Times
Dr. Kathleen Chesto

In this basic yet comprehensive volume of traditional and contemporary prayers, Dr. Chesto shows how to bring family members closer together and closer to God through family prayer and parental involvement. She emphasizes the importance of celebrating and ritualizing key moments of family life, be they standard holidays like Easter and Christmas, or special events within the family, such as the birth of a baby, an engagement, graduation, or learning to ride a bike. Thorough directions are given for the use of prayer and ritual within the family, along with creative suggestions for tailoring rituals and celebrations to each family's particular needs.

ISBN: 0-89622-668-9, 144 pp, $9.95 (order M-53)

Prayers, Activities, Celebrations (and more) for Catholic Families
Bridget Mary Meehan

This creative book introduces parents to a plethora of useful ideas for reinforcing Catholic teachings in the home. Meehan encourages families to come together through exercises and activities which strengthen faith and family ties, improve communication, facilitate prayer, and solidify Catholic values.

ISBN: 0-89622-641-7, 80 pp, $7.95 (order M-38)

Dear God
Prayers for Families with Children
Kathleen Finley

This simple and brief prayer book will help busy families celebrate everyday events like going to school, being in a thunderstorm, and reading together. Also covers church feasts.

ISBN: 0-89622-673-5, 88 pp, $7.95 (order M-52)

Jesus For Children
William Griffin

Each Bible story is told in children's language, retaining the biblical names and the original flavor of the gospel. The large type and full-page illustrations make for easy out-loud reading.

ISBN: 0-89622-610-7, 144 pp, 9.95 (order M-05)

ON VIDEO...

Prayertime, Familytime
Dr. Kathleen Chesto

The author, a religious educator and family expert, speaks directly to parents about family prayer. Citing her own experiences, she assures parents that praying as a family will reap a rich harvest of faith and family unity. She explains how to make family prayer an enjoyable and meaningful daily practice. She helps parents familiarize children with and instill respect for the traditional prayers and prayer forms of the church, develop spontaneous prayer habits, and use prayer to bring new meaning and importance to key moments of family life.

26 minutes, $29.95 (order A-86)

Available at religious bookstores or from:

TWENTY-THIRD PUBLICATIONS
P.O. Box 180 • Mystic, CT 06355

For a complete list of quality books and videos call:
1-800-321-0411